To my Mom, my step-dad, my sister Gabby,
and all of my friends.
And also to an imaginary tiger-sized cat.

Foreword

How many times have you visited your favorite programming forum or mailing list and been amazed at the sheer number of posts on terrain rendering algorithms that seem to fly at you from every angle? Terrain rendering seems to be a favorite subject among today's hobbyist programmers; it serves as an excellent portal to more demanding problems and their solutions. However, terrain rendering is by no means a simple problem, and a particular solution can get rather complex. People from all walks of "programming" life have tried their hand at coming up with the next best solution for rendering their idea of a perfect world. Some even dare say that there are as many terrain rendering algorithms as there are people who write terrain engines. Most of these solutions are variations of more widely accepted solutions. These solutions are generally accepted by people as solutions that give good performance. Some of them have been around for quite a while and have been modified over the years to adapt to the ever-changing hardware they are meant to run on.

This book takes three of these generally accepted solutions and puts them through their paces. I am very pleased to say that one of these solutions came from my very own puddle of programming ideas I have popping up every now and again in a flash of enlightenment. As this book compares three terrain rendering solutions without any prejudice or bias, I am not one to talk about them, obviously. I will leave that to the author.

—Willem H. de Boer

Acknowledgements

Wow, so many people need to be thanked. Let's start with the trademark people: my family and friends. First of all, I want to thank my mom, my step-dad, my sister, and my dog. They rock, and without them, I wouldn't be writing this right now. I'd also like to thank my friends. Thanks to Kyle Way (you owe me) for dealing with me at late times in the night and always distracting me with things. Thanks to Nate, Renae, and Randy for always being there. Also thanks to Luke, Claudia, Amanda, Laurelin, Marissa, Ella, Rebecca, Lacee, Laura, and everyone else. You know who you are!

Next it's time to thank the people I'm not so close to. (In fact, these are the people who are as good of friends as any, but I've never actually seen them before.) First of all, thanks to Evan for being a good programming partner and a good friend. Also thanks to Ron for helping me out a ton and for just being a good guy. Also, a huge thanks to Dave Astle, Kevin Hawkins, and Jeff Molofee for getting me where I am today and being great mentors. Also thanks to Mike, Sean, and Warren for being three really cool guys. I'd also like to give a huge thanks to all the guys in #gamedev who put up with my late-night rants about green bunnies and cats running around my monitor waging war over Christmas lights.

Now, I'd like to thank all the people who made this book possible. A huge thanks goes to Emi Smith, André LaMothe, and Karen Gill for helping to make this book the best it could be, for actually giving me the opportunity to write it, and just generally being a great bunch of people. I'd also like to give another huge thanks to Willem de Boer, Stefan Rottger, and Mark Duchaineau for giving me ideas and reviewing respective chapters to make them the best they could be. In addition, thanks to the people at Longbow Digital Arts for letting me use a demo of *TreadMarks* for this book's CD, the guys at Digital Awe for letting me put *Tropical Storm* on the CD, and the rest of the guys who let me use their demos on the book's CD: Thatcher Ulrich, Leonardo Boselli, and Serba Andrey.

Finally, I'd like to thank the people and things that had no idea they were even involved with this book at all. A huge thanks goes to Fender for making my incredible guitar. Also, Pepsi Corporation deserves a thanks or two for making the legendary Mountain Dew. Another really big thank you goes to the guys at New Found Glory for being a great band and also to Tool, the Offspring, Blink 182, and Nirvana. And finally, thanks to the people at Pacific Sun for providing my "coding clothing."

About the Author

Trent Polack is a high school student currently attending Kalkaska High School. He has been programming in various languages since he was nine years old, when his cousin showed him the joys of QBASIC. Trent is an active contributor to the programming community, contributing several tutorials to GameDev.net and its affiliates. He has a passion for game programming, namely graphics, databases, and, most of all, engine coding. When Trent is not programming, he takes a large interest in reading (especially books by the late Douglas Adams), basketball, playing guitar, and listening to music.

Contents at a Glance

Contents

CHAPTER 6   CLIMBING THE QUADTREE. 105

CHAPTER 7   WHEREVER YOU
MAY ROAM 127

LETTER FROM THE SERIES EDITOR

Sooner or later it had to happen. Someone had to make a game where you could actually go outside and do things other than run around indoors. Don't get me wrong; the age of darkness, the ultimate evil, and the hordes of gruesome creatures around each corner is fun, but we all need some light! *Focus On 3D Terrain Programming* is what that's about.

Everyone (even if you haven't created your own first-person shooter 3D engine) at least has an idea that binary space partitions, octrees, portals, and other similar techniques are usually used for these types of indoor environments. However, the mystique surrounding terrain programming and large-scale outdoor rendering of thousands, hundreds of thousands, or even millions of polygons is still a well-kept trick. Sure, the trick is out there if you read de Boer's geomipmapping algorithm, Rottger's quadtree algorithm, or Duchaineau's ROAM algorithm, but whitepapers with the word *abstract* on them don't appeal to me much. I need something a little more down to earth that actually works in the real world and has code that I can use. This was the motivation for this book.

Focus On 3D Terrain Programming is the first book ever written that focuses on terrain programming 100 percent, and it's the first book that keeps it real and understandable for just about anyone. Moreover, the book is small and cute, and you can buy thousands of copies to create a real 3D terrain if you wish! Seriously though, this book is amazing. The author, Trent Polack, has without a doubt implemented about a zillion terrain engines, and his knowledge, failures, and successes are going to save you a lot of time.

This book starts off assuming you know nothing about terrain programming other than that a computer is going to be involved and you are probably going to need vectors <BG>. Other than that, Trent begins with a general overview of terrain programming and then you start working on your first programs using OpenGL as the API of choice. And don't worry if you're a Direct3D or software 3D guy; OpenGL is like the C/C++ of 3D. It's obvious what's going on, plus it makes all the Linux people happy, which, of course, keep vi sales going strong. In any case, after the introductions are made, the book immediately moves into the various popular terrain algorithms starting from brute force meshing to geomipmapping, quad trees, and ROAM. I'll let you figure out the acronym!

Additionally, texture mapping techniques, lighting, and all the other aspects of rendering the terrains are illustrated with working demos (and there are lots of them). The book finishes up with special effects such as water, mesh animation, particle system (such as for rain), fogging, and bill boarding.

I know I say this a lot, but this is one of my favorite books. What's cool about it is that you can know basically nothing about terrain programming and then in a weekend know just about everything! Plus, Trent's code is some of the nicest I have seen. You can easily follow his logic when concepts in the text are difficult to understand. This is key for programming books because many authors don't have the pages they need to explain something, or it's just a hard subject to discuss. Thus, you are left with the code to bridge the gap, but if the code is "hackeresk," then it's nearly impossible to follow. Trent has gone out of his way to code cleanly, comment often, and use reasonably efficient programming constructs that are optimal but not impossible to understand.

In conclusion, once again, the Premier Game Development Series has made another first with *Focus On 3D Terrain Programming*. I would bet that in a little while, the Internet is going to be flooded with terrain-based 3D games rather than the usual running-around-in-the-dark games, which would be a nice change. I highly recommend this book for anyone who is interested in outdoor 3D rendering and wants to save about 3–6 months with experimenting and learning what has been compressed and filtered into this little jewel of a book.

Sincerely,

André LaMothe
Series Editor for the Premier Game Development Series

Introduction

Welcome to *Focus On 3D Terrain Programming*! This book will take you from a novice programmer with no terrain programming knowledge at all to a fully informed terrain programmer who can implement some of the most complex algorithms around. What exactly is this book about? Well, I'll you.

Focus On 3D Terrain Programming is your answer to 3D terrain programming. It provides comprehensive coverage of the most popular algorithms around (and even one completely new one) and discusses all of their concepts in an easygoing and fun-to-read manner. All explanations are figure heavy for those who like to see an explanation visually rather than try to understand it from text, and explanations are also accompanied by several demos, all of which can be found on the book's companion CD.

Get ready to enter a jungle of terrain-programming goodness; once you enter it, not even the biggest can of Mountain Dew can draw you out. This book moves at a fast pace, but nothing that any C/C++ experienced programmer with some slight knowledge of basic 3D theory will have trouble understanding. No matter how complex a discussion might get, there is always fun to be had, whether it be with a cool new feature to implement or a lame joke. So, without further ado, let's begin the journey!

PART ONE

INTRODUCTION TO TERRAIN PROGRAMMING

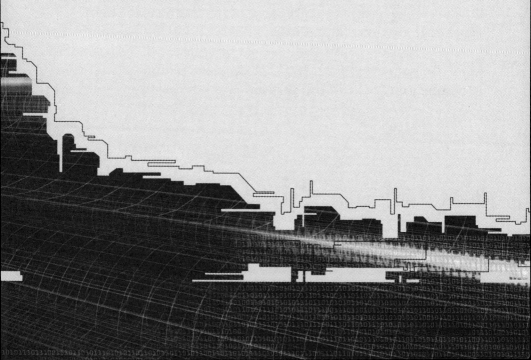

CHAPTER 1

THE JOURNEY INTO THE GREAT OUTDOORS

Welcome to the wonderful world of 3D terrain programming! I'll be your guide through this fun-filled terrain book, and together we'll render the highest mountains, the lowest valleys, and maybe even a blade of grass. Anyway, in this book, you'll learn everything cool there is to learn about terrain programming and its applications to game development. So, pack your bags with your necessities (you know, music, caffeine, socks, and the little teddy bear that you have hidden in the depths of your room) because we're going to get started!

"Terrain? No Thanks, I Already Ate."

I know that the first question you're going to have is this: "What is terrain, anyway?" Well, I'll answer that right off the bat. Terrain is land: rocky mountains, grassy plains, rolling hills, all combining to form a beautiful landscape. The terrain rendering field is concerned with how to render all these magnificent natural features in real-time. After you have the terrain worked out, you need to figure out how to render other features of nature, such as water, clouds, the sun, fog, and other fun stuff.

By the end of this book, you'll fully understand how to create an incredibly realistic outdoor scene that is highly detailed and efficient. Let's do a run-through of some general terrain information, starting with terrain's general (non-game-development based) applications.

General Applications

Before we get to the ultra-cool game-development applications of terrain, let's cover some of the other applications it has. I found a lot of this information at the Virtual Terrain Project[1] (http://www.vterrain.org), which is a great site to find general information on the topic of terrain and all of its applications. Some of the applications of terrain are as follows:

- Virtual tourism (travel planning)
- Visualization of weather and environmental topology
- Real estate walkthroughs
- Military use, such as terrain in a flight simulator (for training purposes)

These are just a few of the many uses for terrain. As you can see, terrain visualization and rendering is an important field of study for several reasons. To truly make terrain rendering a useful tool for a multitude of applications, it must be detailed enough and fast enough to achieve a smooth frame rate. (Sluggish applications completely disturb the realism of any terrain scene, and realism is of the utmost importance.) The information presented here is just the tip of the iceberg; if you're interested in terrain but not game development, check out the wonderful aforementioned site.

Terrain and Game Development

3D terrain has huge applications in game development, especially with the advent of all these nifty, new continuous level of detail (CLOD) algorithms. (The definition of CLOD algorithms is explained later in Chapter 5, "Geomipmapping for the CLOD Impaired.") 3D games were previously impaired by the huge graphical scope of an outdoor-based game. They had a tendency to take place indoors in small rooms and tight hallways. (This was especially common for the first-person shooter genre.)

In the past few years we, as gamers, have seen a series of great outdoor-based games spanning across various genres: strategy, action, and first-person shooters. Games such as *Black and White* (see Figure 1.1) and *Starsiege: Tribes* are two prime examples of outdoor-based games that use terrain extensively.

Of all the outdoor games released in the past few years, one game in particular can take responsibility for the general popularity of 3D terrain in games and as a general topic: *Treadmarks*.

Figure 1.1 *A screenshot from Black and White Studio's Black and White.*

Treadmarks

Released in January 2000, Seamus McNally's *Treadmarks* completely revolutionized the way people think about terrain engines in games and other applications. The game, shown in Figure 1.2, is based on tank combat and racing around a ROAM-based terrain landscape (the details of which will be discussed in Chapter 7, "Wherever You May ROAM") and involves lots of big explosions. The best part about the game is that every shot that is fired affects the landscape. For instance, a normal shell creates a small hole in the landscape, whereas larger weapons have the potential to create a large crater.

Even now, with the game going on three years old, it is still the most impressive display of terrain in any professionally produced game. This is largely due to McNally's implementation of the ROAM algorithm, which displays some new ideas and changes to the algorithm to make it more applicable to a fast-paced graphics application like *Treadmarks* or any other game.

Figure 1.2 *Seamus McNally's* Treadmarks, *a tank combat game that revolution-ized the way people viewed terrain in game development.*

Unfortunately, Seamus McNally lost a three-year battle against Hodgkin's Lymphoma and died on March 30, 2000 at the age of 21. Although I did not know Seamus or his family (the production crew of *Treadmarks*), I'd like to thank him for his incredible ideas and thoughts on terrain visualization and hope that he has found peace. A memorial for him was created at GameDev.net (http://www.gamedev.net/community/memorial/seumas).

Because *Treadmarks* was such a huge milestone for the terrain programming world, I was able to include a demo (from http://www.treadmarks.com) of the game on the book's accompany-ing CD (Demos/TM_16_Demo.exe). I strongly recommend that you check it out now if at all possible. The game has some great terrain effects, and it's a great introduction to what we'll be discussing throughout this book. And it's just such an addicting game!

Demo Building Made Easy!

This book's demos are divided into three groups: the main chapter demos, alternate versions of the main chapter demos, and random demos that various programmers volunteered to include with the book. All of these and more can be found on the book's excellent accompanying CD. I will now go through compilation instructions for the main and alternate book demos. The contributed demos will not be covered; they will be left as a project for you to figure out.

The Main Demos

The main demos are the "official" accompanying demos for each chapter in the book that are coded by yours truly. These demos use OpenGL for the rendering API and custom Windows code, so you can only run them on the Windows operating system. The main demos are also coded in C++ using Microsoft Visual C++ 6.0.

NOTE

It is important to note that although this book's accompanying demos stick to a certain API, the actual text is API and operating-system independent. Whether you use OpenGL, Direct3D, or any other API, you will be able to understand this book's content.

Each chapter's code is divided into two sections: demo code and base code. The demo code is where all of the book's theory and content is implemented into a demo, and the base code contains application initialization, camera routines, math ops, and so on. All are put into a VC++ (Microsoft Visual C++) workspace named demoXX_YY.dsw, where XX is the chapter number and YY is the demo number for the current chapter. When you open up the workspace in VC++, you can just build the application, and it should compile smoothly. Let's implement this with a step by step for demo1_1, which you can find on the accompanying CD under Code\Chapter 1\demo1_1.

First, open Microsoft Visual C++ and demo1_1.dsw (File, Open Workspace). After you do that, the project toolbar should look like Figure 1.3.

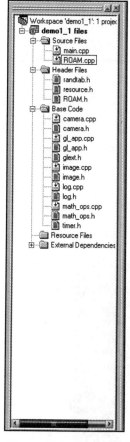

Figure 1.3 *Project toolbar for demo1_1 In Microsoft Visual C++ 6.0.*

From there, you can simply build (Build, Build demo1_1.exe) the demo and then execute the EXE. The demo is almost an exact replica of demo7_1 (Chapter 7's first demo), so you can expect to see something similar later on in the book. For now though, a quick explanation will do. The demo shows what a simple tessellation of the ROAM algorithm looks like. Now that you've had that little teaser, just wait until you get to the rather large Chapter 7! If you build demo1_1 correctly, it should look like Figure 1.4. Also take a look at the controls for the demo in Table 1.1.

Table 1.1   Controls for demo1_1

Key	Function
Escape / Q	Quit the program
Up arrow	Move forward
Down arrow	Move backward
Right arrow	Strafe right
Left arrow	Strafe left

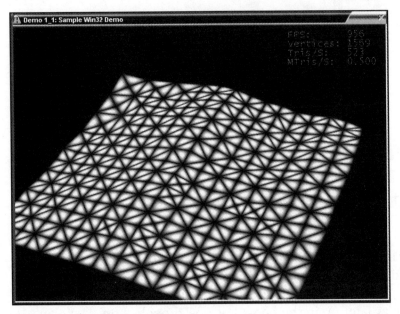

Figure 1.4 *Screenshot of demo1_1.*

Isn't that a beautiful screenshot? I think so. Anyway, that's a lame example of what we will be accomplishing in this book, but it works for a little teaser!

The Book at an Itty-Bitty Glance

This book will be about terrain, terrain, terrain, and *gasp* even MORE terrain! We'll cover everything from fractal heightmap generation to three different CLOD algorithms. We'll end with a tremendously large chapter on special effects that can be used to increase the realism and detail of any 3D terrain scene. These effects consist of such things as fog, cloud rendering, lens flares, and other various tips, tricks, and effects. So, without further ado, let's get to the summary. We'll take the book part-by-part instead of chapter-by-chapter.

Part One: Introduction to Terrain Programming

This Part eases you into terrain programming. Chapter 2, "Terrain 101," discusses heightmap ops, such as loading and saving heightmaps, and then continues on to discuss generating a heightmap. (A heightmap is a 2D image that defines the height for every vertex in a terrain engine.) The heightmap generation section is really neat because it teaches you how to create cool-looking heightmaps with little work.

Chapter 3, "Texturing Terrain," starts off with stretching a single texture across a terrain mesh. From there, the chapter moves on to discuss procedural texture generation, which produces much better-looking results than stretching a single grass or dirt texture. The chapter then adds what is called a detail texture to the terrain, which greatly improves the visual appearance of the landscape.

Chapter 4, "Lighting Terrain," is the final chapter for Part One. It covers simplistic terrain lighting techniques. Starting off with the incredibly simple height-based terrain lighting, the chapter then continues on to lightmapping terrain. The chapter closes with the incredibly awesome slope-lighting technique, which provides great lighting with a minimal amount of code.

Part Two: Advanced Terrain Programming

Chapters 5, "Geomipmapping for the CLOD Impaired," 6, "Climbing the Quadtree," and 7, "Wherever You May ROAM," deal with CLOD-based terrain algorithms. A CLOD algorithm, in one sentence, is a dynamic polygonal mesh that "gives" extra triangles to areas that require more detail. That's a simplistic explanation of the matter, but it will work until we get further into the book. Following are the algorithms that are covered:

- Willem H. de Boer's geomipmapping algorithm
- Stefan Roettger's quadtree algorithm
- Mark Duchaineau's ROAM algorithm

What exactly these are will be explained in time, but briefly: They are *really* cool! Each one is great in its own way, and each is completely different from the others, which makes for a rather varied coding experience later on. Chapters 5, 6, and 7 are going to be a blast for you to read through. We will then end the book with a wide variety of special effects and tricks to "spice up" the previously mentioned implementations in Chapter 8, "Wrapping It Up: Special Effects and More." In that chapter, we will be covering cool effects such as fog, deformation, and other "environmental" effects.

The Demos

I have programmed a demo for every major topic that is discussed throughout this book. As we proceed through the book, it is imperative that you keep in mind that the demos I provide are *only* to be used as a stepping stone for your own implementation. My implementations are made to be a good teaching guide for you to base your demos off of; don't just copy and paste the demo code into your own project. The demos provided are not highly optimized, do not provide optimal detail, and do not implement all the bells and whistles of the various techniques we will be discussing.

Because I'm such a nice guy, I decided to help you out a bit. Terrain is a dynamic issue: The techniques that work one day might need to be completely overhauled to be useful another day. Therefore, I have dedicated most of my site (http://trent.codershq.com/) to terrain research and implementation, and I will be keeping a constant database of my progress in the field of 3D terrain programming. I will attempt to develop the most detailed and speediest implementations that I can, and I will keep a constant log of the developments that I make. If the demos that are provided on the book's CD just aren't enough for you, be sure to check out my site for a series of demos and information that will serve as an invaluable companion to this book.

Summary

This chapter covered the basics of terrain and its applications. It also looked at how to compile and execute two different types of demos and provided an overview of the entire book. Get ready: Your journey through the wonderful world of terrain rendering is about to begin!

CHAPTER 2

TERRAIN 101

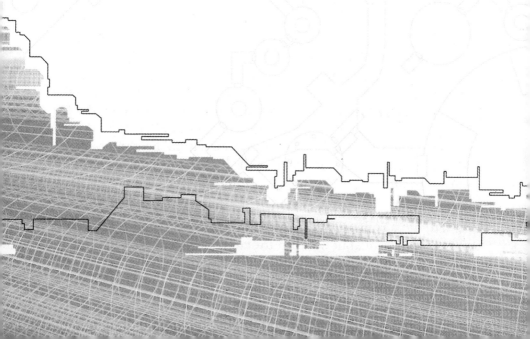

Well, here it is—your first real introduction into the world of 3D terrain programming! This chapter will cover all the aspects of terrain rendering that you need to know before you start having fun with texturing/lighting techniques, as well as various "hardcore" terrain algorithms. In this chapter, you will learn the following key concepts:

- What heightmaps are, how to create them, and how to load them
- How to render terrain using a brute force algorithm
- How to generate fractal terrain using two algorithms: fault formation and midpoint displacement

So, without further ado, let's get started!

Heightmaps

Imagine that you have a regular grid of polygons that extends along the X and Z axes. In case you don't know what I'm talking about, Figure 2.1 might refresh your memory.

Now that's a pretty boring image! How exactly are we going to go about making it more, well, terrain-ish? The answer is by using a heightmap. A heightmap, in our case, is a series of `unsigned char` variables (which let us have values in the range of 0–255, which happens to be the number of shades of gray in a grayscale image) that we will be creating at run-time or in a paint program. This heightmap defines the height values for our terrain, so if we have our grid along the X and Z axes, the heightmap defines the values that will extend the grid into the Y axis. For a quick example, check out the heightmap in Figure 2.2. After we load it in and apply it to our terrain, the grid in Figure 2.1 will transform into the beautiful terrain (although it is extremely lacking in color and lighting) that you see in Figure 2.3.

Granted, the terrain in Figure 2.3 looks pretty boring without cool textures or lighting, but we need to start somewhere! As I was just explaining, heightmaps give us the power to shape a boring grid of vertices into a magnificent landscape. The question is, what exactly is

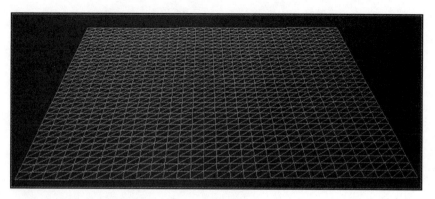

Figure 2.1 *A grid of vertices with non-defined height values.*

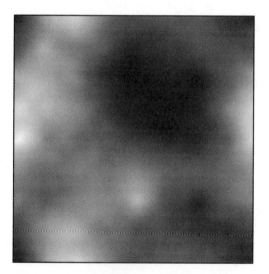

Figure 2.2 *The 128 × 128 heightmap used to create Figure 2.3.*

a heightmap? Normally, a heightmap is a grayscale image in which
each pixel represents a height value. (In our case, the height ranges
from 0–255, the number of shades of gray in a grayscale image.) Dark
colors represent a lower elevation, and lighter colors represent a
higher elevation. Refer to Figures 2.2 and 2.3; notice how the 3D
terrain (Figure 2.3) corresponds exactly to the heightmap in Figure
2.2, with everything from the peaks, to the valleys, and even the
colors? That is what we want our heightmaps to do: Give us the power
to "mold" a grid of vertices to create the terrain that we want.

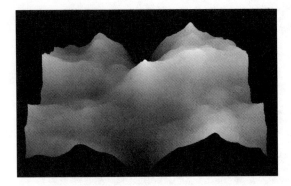

Figure 2.3 *Brute force terrain image created by using the heightmap in Figure 2.2.*

In our case, the file format for our heightmaps is going to be in the RAW format. (Although most of the demos create heightmaps dynamically, I included the option to save/load heightmaps using the RAW format.) I chose this format simply because it is incredibly simple to use. In addition, because the RAW format contains only *pure* data, it is easier to load the heightmap in. (We also are loading in a grayscale RAW image, which makes things even easier.) Before we load a RAW image, we need to do a couple of things. First, we need to create a simple data structure that can represent a heightmap. What we need for this structure is a buffer of unsigned char variables (we need to be able to allocate the memory dynamically) and a variable to keep track of the heightmap's size. Simple enough, eh? Well, here it is:

```
struct SHEIGHT_DATA
{
    unsigned char* m_pucData; //the height data
    int m_iSize;              //the height size (power of 2)
};
```

The Creation of a Base Terrain Class

We need to create a base class from which all of our specific terrain engines (brute force, geomipmapping, and so on) will be derived. We do not want the user to actually create an instance of this class; we just want this class to be the common parent for our specific implementations that we'll develop later. See Figure 2.4 to get a visual idea of what I have in mind.

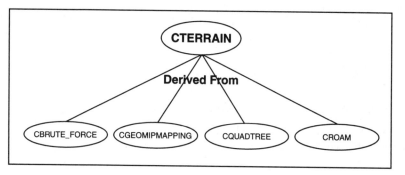

Figure 2.4 *The relationship between* CTERRAIN *and the four terrain implementations.*

NOTE

The CTERRAIN class is what us C++ junkies like to refer to as an abstract class. An abstract class is a class that functions as a common interface for all of its children. Think of it this way: A mother has red hair but has a boring personality. Although all of her children have inherited the mother's red hair, each has a distinct personality that is incredibly entertaining. The same applies to an abstract class; although an abstract class is "boring" by itself, its traits carry on to its children, and those children can define more "exciting" behavior for themselves.

So far, all that we need in our base class is three variables: an instance of SHEIGHT_DATA, a height scaling variable (which will let us dynamically scale the heights of our terrain), and a size variable (which should be the same as the size member of SHEIGHI_DATA). As far as functions go, we need some heightmap manipulation functions and a function to set the height scaling variable. Here's what I came up with:

```
class CTERRAIN
{
    protected:
        SHEIGHT_DATA m_heightData;  //the height data
```

```
      float m_fHeightScale;          //scaling variable

public:
      int m_iSize;                          //must be a power of two


virtual void Render( void )= 0;

bool LoadHeightMap( char* szFilename, int iSize );
bool SaveHeightMap( char* szFilename );
bool UnloadHeightMap( void );


//------------------------------------
// Name:         SetHeightScale - public
// Description:  Set the height scaling variable
// Arguments:    -fScale: how much to scale the terrain
// Return Value: None
//------------------------------------
inline void SetHeightScale( float fScale )
{     m_fHeightScale= fScale;     }


//------------------------------------
// Name:         SetHeightAtPoint - public
// Description:  Set the true height value at the given point
// Arguments:    -ucHeight: the new height value for the point
//               -iX, iZ: which height value to retrieve
// Return Value: None
//------------------------------------
inline void SetHeightAtPoint( unsigned char ucHeight,
                              int iX, int iZ)
{     m_heightData.m_pucData[( iZ*m_iSize )+iX]= ucHeight;     }


//------------------------------------
// Name:         GetTrueHeightAtPoint - public
// Description:  A function to get the true height
//               value (0-255) at a point
// Arguments:    -iX, iZ: which height value to retrieve
// Return Value: An unsigned char value: the true height at
//               the given point
```

```
//-------------------------------------
inline unsigned char GetTrueHeightAtPoint( int iX, int iZ )
{    return ( m_heightData.m_pucData[( iZ*m_iSize )+iX );    }



//-------------------------------------
// Name:          GetScaledHeightAtPoint - public
// Description:   Retrieve the scaled height at a given point
// Arguments:     -iX, iZ: which height value to retrieve
// Return Value:  A float value: the scaled height at the given
//                 point
//-------------------------------------
inline float GetScaledHeightAtPoint( int iX, int iZ )
{ return ( ( m_heightData.m_pucData[( iZ*m_iSize )+iX]
          )*m_fHeightScale ); }

CTERRAIN( void )
{    }
~CTERRAIN( void )
{    }
};
```

Not too shabby if I do say so myself! Well that's our "parent" terrain
class! Every other implementation we develop derives from this class.
I put quite a few heightmap manipulation functions in the class just to
make things easier both for us and for the users. I included two height
retrieval functions for a reason. Whereas we, as the developers, will use
the "true" function the most often, the user will be using the "scaled"
function the most often to perform collision detection (which we will
be doing in Chapter 8, "Wrapping It Up: Special Effects and More").

Loading and Unloading
a Heightmap

I've been talking about both of these routines for a while now, and it's
about time that we finally dive straight into them. These routines are
simple, so don't make them any harder than they should be. We are
just doing some simple C-Style File I/O.

We need to talk about how to load, save, and unload a heightmap. The best place to start is with the loading routine because you cannot unload something without it being loaded. We need two arguments for the function: the file name and the size of the map. Inside the function, we want to make a FILE instance so that we can load the requested heightmap. Then we want to make sure that the class's heightmap instance is not already loaded with information; if it is, then we need to call the unloading routine and continue about our business. Here is the code for what we just discussed:

```
bool CTERRAIN::LoadHeightMap( char* szFilename, int iSize )
{
    FILE* pFile;

    //check to see if the data has been set
    if( m_heightData.m_pucData )
        UnloadHeightMap( );
```

Next, we need to open the file and allocate memory in our heightmap instance's data buffer (m_heightData.m_pucData). We need to make sure that the memory was allocated correctly and that something didn't go horribly wrong.

```
    //allocate the memory for our height data
    m_heightData.m_pucData= new unsigned char [iSize*iSize];

    //check to see whether the memory was successfully allocated
    if( m_heightData.m_pucData==NULL )
    {
        //the memory could not be allocated
        //something is seriously wrong here
        printf( "Could not allocate memory for%s\n", szFilename );
```

```
        return false;
    }
```

For the next-to-last step in our loading process, we are going to load the actual data and place it in our heightmap instance's data buffer. Then we are going to close the file, set some of the class's member variables, and print a success message.

```
    //read the heightmap into context
    fread( m_heightData.m_pucData, 1, iSize*iSize, pFile );

    //close the file
    fclose( pFile );

    //set the size data
    m_heightData.m_iSize= iSize;
    m_iSize              = m_heightData.m_iSize;

    //Yahoo! The heightmap has been successfully loaded!
    printf( "Loaded %s\n", szFilename );
    return true;
}
```

> **NOTE**
>
> The heightmap saving routine is almost the same thing as the loading routine. Basically, we just need to replace fread with fwrite. That's all there is to it!

That's it for the loading routine. Let's move on to the unloading routine before I lose your attention. The unloading procedures are simple. We just have to check whether the memory has actually been allocated, and if it has, we need to delete it.

```
bool CTERRAIN::UnloadHeightMap( void )
{
    //check to see if the data has been set
    if( m_heightData.m_pucData )
    {
        //delete the data
        delete[] m_heightData.m_pucData;
```

```
            //reset the map dimensions, also
            m_heightData.m_iSize= 0;
      }


      //the heightmap has been unloaded
      printf( "Successfully unloaded the heightmap\n" );
      return true;
}
```

I really do not need to check to see whether the data buffer is a NULL
pointer (delete internally checks whether the pointer is NULL), so my
check is a bit redundant. The check is a habit that I've gotten into,
however, so I'll be doing it throughout this book. Just know that you
can call delete without checking for a NULL pointer first. Now it's
about time that I showed you a simple way of rendering what we have
just been talking about.

The Brute Force
of the Matter

Rendering terrain using a brute force algorithm is incredibly simple,
and it provides the highest amount of detail possible. Unfortunately, it
is the slowest of all of the algorithms that this book presents. Basically,
if you have a heightmap of 64 × 64 pixels, then the terrain, when rendered using brute force, consists of 64 × 64 vertices, in a regular
repeating pattern (see Figure 2.5).

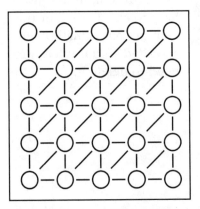

Figure 2.5 A 5 × 5 patch of brute force terrain vertices.

In case you didn't immediately recognize it, we will be rendering each row of vertices as a triangle strip because this is the most logical way to render the vertices. You wouldn't exactly want to render them as individual triangles or as triangle fans with a structure like the one presented in Figure 2.5, would you?

For this chapter's demo, I'm keeping things as simple as possible. The color for the vertex will be based on its height, so all vertices will be shades of gray. And that's all there is to rendering terrain using brute force. Here is a quick snippet using OpenGL to show how we will be rendering the terrain:

```
void CBRUTE_FORCE::Render( void )
{
    unsigned char ucColor;
    int iZ;
    int iX;

    //loop through the Z axis of the terrain
    for( iZ=0; iZ<m_iSize-1; iZ++ )
    {
        //begin a new triangle strip
        glBegin( GL_TRIANGLE_STRIP );

        //loop through the X axis of the terrain
        //this is where the triangle strip is constructed
        for( iX=0; iX<m_iSize-1; iX++ )
        {
            //Use height-based coloring. (High-points are
            //light, and low points are dark.)
            ucColor= GetTrueHeightAtPoint( iX, iZ );

            //set the color with OpenGL, and render the point
            glColor3ub( ucColor, ucColor, ucColor );
            glVertex3f( iX, GetScaledHeightAtPoint( iX, iZ ), iZ );

            //Use height-based coloring. (High-points are
            //light, and low points are dark.)
            ucColor= GetTrueHeightAtPoint( iX, iZ+1 );
```

```
            //set the color with OpenGL, and render the point
            glColor3ub( ucColor, ucColor, ucColor );
            glVertex3f( iX,
                        GetScaledHeightAtPoint( iX, iZ+1 ),
                        iZ+1 );
        }


        //end the triangle strip
        glEnd( );
    }
}
```

It's time for your first actual demo that *you* created! Check out
demo2_1 on the CD. Go to Code\Chapter 2\demo2_1, open up the
workspace in Microsoft Visual C++, and starting having fun! The demo
shows everything that we have just been discussing. Figure 2.6 shows a
screenshot of the demo, and Table 2.1 provides a description of the
controls for the demo. To move your viewpoint, just hold down the
left or right mouse button and drag the mouse.

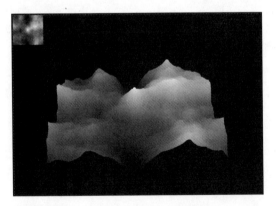

Figure 2.6 *A screenshot from demo2_1.*

Woohoo! Now, I said a while back that we were going to be creating
most of our heightmaps dynamically. You might be asking yourself,
"How do I do that?" Well, I'm glad you asked. (And even if you didn't,
I'm still going to explain it!) Now we are going to learn how to procedurally generate heightmaps using two fractal terrain generation techniques. Get ready!

Table 2.1 Controls for demo 2_1

Key	Function
Escape / Q	Quit the program
Up arrow	Move forward
Down arrow	Move backward
Right arrow	Strafe right
Left arrow	Strafe left
W	Render in wireframe mode
S	Render in solid/fill mode
+ / -	Increase/decrease mouse sensitivity
] / [	Increase/decrease movement sensitivity

Fractal Terrain Generation

Fractal terrain generation is the process of algorithmically generating terrain, although in our case, we are simply generating a heightmap to be used as the "blueprint" for our terrain. We will be going through two algorithms here, the first of which is fault formation and the second of which is midpoint displacement. We will be using the fault formation algorithm through most of the book because it does not place a restriction on what dimensions must be used for the generated heightmap, whereas midpoint displacement requires that the dimensions be a power of two. (The dimensions must also be equal, so although you can generate a heightmap of 1024×1024, you cannot generate a heightmap of 512×1024.) So, without further delay, let's get started with the fractal terrain generation algorithms!

Fault Formation

One method of fractal terrain generation is called *fault formation*. Fault formation is the process of generating "faults" in terrain; for the most part, it produces fairly smooth terrain. Basically, all we do is add a random line to a blank height field, and then we add a random height to one of the sides. See Figure 2.7 if you are having trouble visualizing this or if you just want a confirmation that the image in your head (or, if you're like me, the voice in your head—I'm strange like that) is correct.

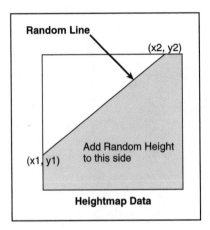

Figure 2.7 *The first step in the fault-formation algorithm.*

That's just the first step in the entire process, of course. There are still some things you need to know about the algorithm before you reach the advanced stages of it. First, the height value that I talked about earlier needs to be decreased with every iteration. Why, you might ask? Well, if you didn't decrease the height after each pass, you'd end up with a heightmap like Figure 2.8. See Figure 2.9 for examples of what the heightmaps *should* look like.

Notice, in Figure 2.8, how the light/dark spots have no rhyme or reason; they are just spread out all over the place. This would be fine for chaotic terrain, but we want to create smooth, rolling hills. Have no fear; fixing this problem is rather simple. We want to linearly decrease the height value without having it drop to zero. To do this, we use the following equation (taken from demo2_2):

```
iHeight= iMaxDelta - ( ( iMaxDelta-iMinDelta )*iCurrentIteration
)/iIterations;
```

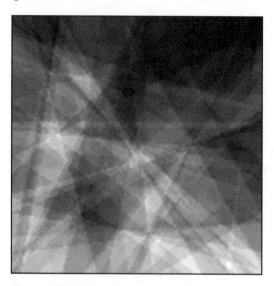

Figure 2.8 *A map generated with completely random height values.*

iMinDelta, iMaxDelta, and iIterations are all provided as function arguments. iMinDelta and iMaxDelta represent the lowest and highest (respectively) values that you want for the height when forming new faults. I tend to stick with a value of 0 for iMinDelta and a value of 255 for iMaxDelta. iIterations, as I said before, represents the number of fault passes to make (how many different times the heightmap should be divided). And last, but certainly not least, iCurrentIteration represents the current iteration number.

As I said earlier, we only want to elevate one side of the line, and we want to raise the height value of every point on that side of the line. Therefore, we're going to have to loop through all of the height values for the entire heightmap. All of this is easy to accomplish; it just involves some simple math. We have a vector that goes in the direction of our line (which is defined by the two random points that we created earlier), and its direction is stored in (iDirX1, iDirZ1). The next vector that we want to create is a vector from the initial random point (iRandX1, iRandZ1) to the current point in the loop (x, z). After that is done, we need to find the Z component of the cross product, and if it is greater than zero, then we need to elevate the current point in question. All of the previous explanation is shown next in code from the demo.

```
//iDirX1, iDirZ1 is a vector going the same direction as the line
iDirX1= iRandX2-iRandX1;
iDirZ1= iRandZ2-iRandZ1;

for( x=0; x<m_iSize; x++ )
{
    for( z=0; z<m_iSize; z++ )
    {
    //iDirX2, iDirZ2 is a vector from iRandX1, iRandZ1 to the
    //current point (in the loop).
    iDirX2= x-iRandX1;
    iDirZ2= z-iRandZ1;

    //if the result of ( iDirX2*iDirZ1 - iDirX1*iDirZ2 ) is "up"
    //(above 0), then raise this point by iHeight
    if( ( iDirX2*iDirZ1 - iDirX1*iDirZ2 )>0 )
        fTempBuffer[( z*m_iSize )+x]+= ( float )iHeight;
    }
}
```

NOTE

While you're looking at the fault formation and midpoint displacement code in these two segments and in demo2_2, you might notice how I create a temporary buffer, fTempBuffer, of floating point values to stick all of the height values in. If you remember, though, I talked about our heightmaps being an array of unsigned char variables. Why would I use floating-point variables in this situation? I did this because the algorithm needed a higher degree of accuracy than our normal unsigned char height buffer. After we have the entire heightmap created and normalized, I transfer all of the information from fTempBuffer to the height buffer in the CTERRAIN class, m_heightData.

Check out Figure 2.9 to see several heightmaps formed using fault formation and a varying number of fault-line iterations.

As close as we are, we are not finished with this algorithm yet! In case you didn't notice, the maps in the previous figure looked non-terrainish (new word). We need to pass an *erosion filter* over the entire map

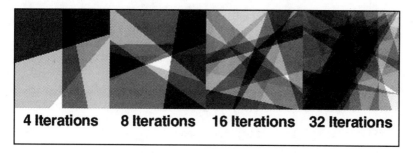

4 Iterations   8 Iterations   16 Iterations   32 Iterations

Figure 2.9 *Examples of heightmaps created after several "fault formation" passes.*

after we form a new fault to smooth out the values that we have. This process is very much, if not exactly, like passing a blur filter over an image in your favorite paint program. If it helps you to understand the following explanation, just think of it like that.

What we are going to be doing is applying a simple FIR filter, as suggested by Jason Shankel.[1] This filter is meant to simulate terrain erosion, which happens frequently in nature. (Have you ever seen a series of mountains in nature that looked like the heightmaps in Figure 2.9?) We are going to be taking data in bands, rather than filtering the whole heightmap at once. The filtering function looks like this:

```
void CTERRAIN::FilterHeightBand( float* fpBand, int iStride,
                                 int iCount, float fFilter )
{
    float v= ucpBand[0];
    int j  = iStride;
    int i;

    //Go through the height band and apply the erosion filter
    for( i=0; i<iCount-1; i++ )
    {
        ucpBand[j]= fFilter*v + ( 1-fFilter )*ucpBand[j];

        v = ucpBand[j];
        j+= iStride;
    }
}
```

This function takes a single band of height values and goes through them value by value, with iStride dictating how much to advance the values by for each iteration in the loop. iStride also dictates which direction to go because we'll be filtering the entire height field from top to bottom, bottom to top, left to right, and right to left. The most important line of the entire function is this one:

```
ucpBand[j]= fFilter*v + ( 1-fFilter )*ucpBand[j];
```

This is the line that blurs/erodes. Various values for fFilter affect blurring. 0.0f is no blurring at all, and 1.0f is a really strong blur. Usually, we want values to be in the range of 0.3f to 0.6f, depending on how smooth you want the terrain to be. Now, for instance, let's say we had a filter value of 0.25f, and the current band value was 0.9f. The previous equation would look like this:

```
ucpBand[j]= 0.25f*v + ( 1-0.25f )*0.9f;
```

After we perform the initial calculations, the previous equation would simplify down to this:

```
ucpBand[j]= 0.25f*v + 0.675f;
```

0.675f is the new value for the heightmap pixel that we are blurring, but now it needs to be interpolated with the pixel before it. (We'll give that pixel a value of 0.87f.) We apply the 0.25f blurring filter value to that pixel and add it to the uninterpolated pixel value for the pixel that we are trying to calculate:

```
ucpBand[j]= 0.25f*0.87f + 0.675f;
```

Doing the final calculations, we end up with a value of 0.8925f. So, you see, all we are really doing here is "mixing" a bit of the previous pixel with the current pixel. Check out Figure 2.10 to see how filtering looks on a much larger scale than the per-pixel operations we were previously talking about.

Play around with demo2_2 a bit. I made a new area of the menu for heightmap manipulation, and now you can create new heightmaps dynamically. If you find one you like, just select the Save Current option, and the heightmap will be saved to the program's directory. When you select the Fault Formation option, a dialog box opens up and prompts you to enter a value for detail. This value is an integer value, so keep the numbers in the range of 0–100 for this. Now, it's time for some midpoint displacement fun!

Figure 2.10 *Heightmaps that were generated using the fault-formation algorithm and the erosion filter. The top image has a filter value of 0.0f, the middle image has a filter value of 0.2f, and the bottom image has a filter value of 0.4f.*

Midpoint Displacement

Fault formation works great for a nice little scene composed of some small hills, but what if you want something more chaotic than that, such as a mountain range? Well, look no further. *Midpoint displacement²* is the answer that you're looking for! This algorithm is also known as the plasma fractal and the diamond-square algorithm. However, midpoint displacement sounds so much cooler, and it gives the reader (that's you) a better idea of what actually is going on in this whole process, so I'll stick to that term most of the time.

All we are doing in this algorithm, essentially, is taking a single line's midpoint and displacing it! Let me give you a one-dimensional run-through. If we had a simple line, such as AB in Figure 2.11, we'd take its midpoint, represented as C in the figure, and move it!

> **NOTE**
>
> It's important to note that the midpoint displacement algorithm has a slight drawback to it: The algorithm can only generate square heightmaps, and the dimensions have to be a power of two. This is unlike the fault formation algorithm, in which you can specify any dimension that you want.

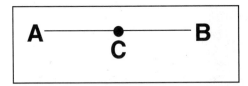

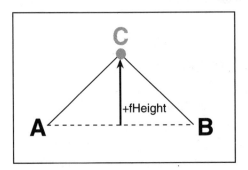

Figure 2.11 *A simple line, which is the first stage in the 1D version of the algorithm.*

Now, we're going to displace the midpoint of that line by a height value, which we'll call fHeight (see Figure 2.12). We'll make it equivalent to the length of the line in question, and we'll displace the midpoint by a range of -fHeight/2 to fHeight/2. (We want to subdivide the line in two each time, and we want to displace the height of the line somewhere in that range.)

Figure 2.12 *The line from Figure 2.11 after one displacement pass.*

After the first pass, we need to decrease the value of fHeight to achieve the roughness that we desire. To do this, we simply multiply fHeight by $2^{-fRoughness}$, in which fRoughness is a constant that represents the desired roughness of the terrain. The user will specify the value for fRoughness, so you need to know a bit about the various values you can put for it. The value can, technically, be any floating-point value that your heart desires, but the best results are from 0.25f to 1.5f. Check out Figure 2.13 for a visual indicator of what varying levels of roughness can do.

As you can see, the value you pass for fRoughness greatly influences the look of the heightmap. Values that are lower than 1.0f create chaotic terrain, values of 1.0f create a fairly "balanced" look, and values that

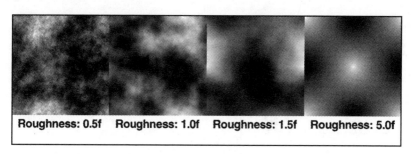

| Roughness: 0.5f | Roughness: 1.0f | Roughness: 1.5f | Roughness: 5.0f |

Figure 2.13 *Varying values pass for* fRoughness.

are greater than 1.0f create smooth terrain. Now, let's kick this explanation into the second dimension.

Keep the 1D explanation in your head constantly as we talk about what to change for the 2D explanation because every concept you just learned for that single line still applies. The exception is that, instead of calculating the midpoint for a single line, we now have to calculate the midpoints for four different lines, average them, and then add the height value in the middle of the square. Figure 2.14 shows the blank square (ABCD) that we start with.

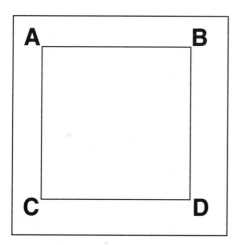

Figure 2.14 *The first stage in the 2D version of the algorithm. (No displacement has occurred yet.)*

As I said a second ago, we have to calculate the midpoint for all four lines (AB, BD, DC, CA). The resulting point, E, should be directly in the middle of the square. We then displace E by taking the average of A, B, C, and D's height values, and then we add a random value in the range of -fHeight/2 to fHeight/2. This results in the image shown in Figure 2.15.

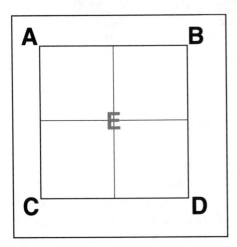

Figure 2.15 *The first-half displacement stage in the 2D version of the algorithm.*

That was only the first half of the first displacement stage. Now we have to calculate the height values for each of the midpoints that we found earlier. This is similar to what we did before, though; we just average the height values of the surrounding vertices and add a random height value in the range of -fHeight/2 to fHeight/2. You end up with a square like that shown in Figure 2.16.

You then recourse down to the next set of rectangles and perform the same process. If you understand the 1D explanation, however, you are certain to understand the 2D explanation and the accompanying code, demo2_2, found on the CD under Code\Chapter 2\demo2_2. Compiling information, as usual, is supplied as a text file in the demo's directory. Go check out the demo. Controls are the same as the last time (see Table 2.1 for a reminder), but this time, when you click Midpoint Displacement for the Detail field, you want values in the range of 0 (*really* chaotic terrain) to 150 (simple terrain). Have fun!

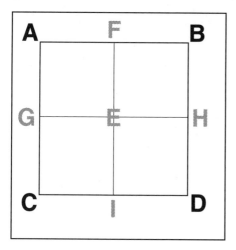

Figure 2.16 *The final step in the first displacement stage.*

Summary

In this chapter, you received your introductory degree into terrain programming. You learned all about heightmaps: what they are, how to generate them, and how to load/unload them. Then you learned how to render those heightmaps using brute force, the simplest (and best looking) terrain algorithm on the market. Finally, you learned two ways to procedurally generate a heightmap for the terrain. In the next two chapters, we'll learn all about "spicing up" our terrain with cool texturing and lighting techniques.

References

1 Shankel, Jason. "Fractal Terrain Generation—Fault Formation." *Game Programming Gems.* Rockland, Massachusetts: Charles River Media, 2000. 499–502.

2 Shankel, Jason. "Fractal Terrain Generation—Midpoint Displacement." *Game Programming Gems.* Rockland, Massachusetts: Charles River Media, 2000. 503–507.

CHAPTER 3

TEXTURING TERRAIN

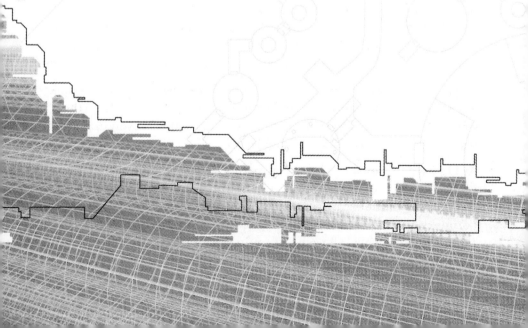

Now that you've had your introduction to making a simple terrain mesh, you need to know how to add detail to that boring ol' mesh using a texture map. I'm going to keep this discussion about texturing simple and straight to the point so that we can get started with the really fun stuff (the terrain algorithms). I'm going to quit wasting space now and just tell you what you are going to be learning in this chapter:

- How to apply a large single-pattern texture map to a terrain mesh
- How to procedurally generate a complex texture map using various terrain "tiles"
- How to add a detail texture to the terrain to add even more detail to the previously generated textures

Simple Texture Mapping

We are going to start with some simple texture mapping. You will learn how to "stretch" one texture over an entire terrain mesh. Most of the time, this technique looks *really* bad unless, of course, you have a really well-made texture map, which is what we are going to work on in the next section. What counts right now is that you learn *how* to stretch the texture without regard to what the end result will look like.

To stretch a single texture across the landscape, we are going to make every vertex in the landscape fall within the range of 0.0f–1.0f (the standard range for texture coordinates). Doing this is even easier than it sounds. To start out, look at Figure 3.1.

As Figure 3.1 shows, the lower-left corner of the terrain mesh (for example purposes, we'll choose a heightmap resolution of 256 × 256), (0,0) would have texture coordinates of (0.0f, 0.0f), and the upper-left corner of the terrain (255, 255), would have texture coordinates of (1.0f, 1.0f). Basically, all we need to do is find out which vertex we are currently rendering and divide it by the heightmap resolution. (Doing

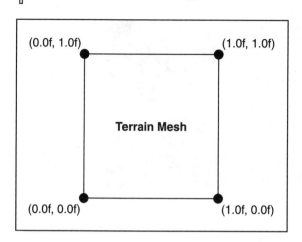

Figure 3.1 *Texture coordinates over a terrain mesh.*

so produces values in the range that we want, 0.0f–1.0f, without having us step over our boundary. This is important to note because we *do* want to step out of the previously mentioned range in a later section.) Before we render each vertex, we need to calculate three things: texture values for x, z, and z+1, which I will call fTexLeft, fTexBottom, and fTexTop, respectively. Here is how we calculate the values:

```
fTexLeft   = ( float )x/m_iSize;
fTexBottom= ( float )z/m_iSize;
fTexTop    = ( float )( z+1 )/m_iSize;
```

And to think you thought this was going to be hard! Anyway, we need to do the previous calculations for each vertex that we render and then send the texture coordinates to our rendering API. When we render the vertex (x, z), we send (fTexLeft, fTexBottom) as our texture coordinates, and when we render (x, z+1), we send (fTexLeft, fTexTop) as our texture coordinates. Check out Figure 3.2 and demo3_1 on the CD in Code\Chapter 3\demo3_1 to see the fruits of your labor.

The screenshot has more detail than our landscapes in Chapter 2, "Terrain 101" (notice that I removed shading, however), but it's hard to discern the actual form of the landscape. Stretching a simple texture (see Figure 3.3), even if the texture used in demo3_1 is at a rather high resolution, fails to capture the amount of detail that we would like to have in our texture map.

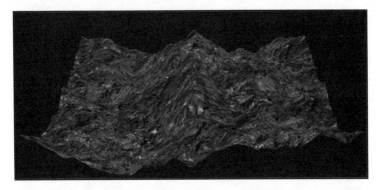

Figure 3.2 *Screenshot from demo3_1.*

Figure 3.3 *The grass texture used in demo3_1.*

We need more detail. We want a texture map similar to the one in Figure 3.4, which was procedurally generated using a series of texture "tiles" (dirt, grass, rock, and snow in this case).

See how much detail is shown in the texture of Figure 3.4? The texturing of this figure helps distinguish tall mountainous areas from low plain areas a lot better than the single grass texture shown in Figure 3.3. You need to know how to generate a really cool texture like the one shown here. Read on!

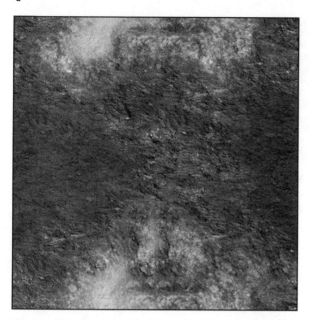

Figure 3.4 *The type of texture that we want to use for our demos.*

Procedural Texture Generation

Procedural texture generation is a cool and useful technique that is a great addition to any terrain engine. After we finish our procedural texture generator, we are going to have the user load a series of two to four tiles of his choice. Then we are going to call our texture-generating function. (All the user has to know is the size of the texture that he wants to be created.) That's it! How do we go about creating our texture-generation function? First, you need to know what our actual goal is here. We are going to be using the terrain's heightmap to generate a texture that will coincide with it. We will go through each pixel of our texture map, finding the height that corresponds to that pixel and figuring out each texture tile's presence at that pixel. (Each tile has a "region" structure that defines its areas of influence.) Very rarely will a tile be 100% visible at a pixel, so we need to "combine" that tile with the rest of the other tiles (interpolating the RGB color values). The result will look something like it does in Figure 3.5, where you can see what the interpolation would look like between a grass and a rock tile.

Figure 3.5 *A segment from the texture map in Figure 3.4, which shows the interpolation between a rock and a grass tile.*

The Region System

To start coding the previously mentioned procedure, we need to start by creating a structure to hold the region information for each tile. A *region*, as it applies here, is a series of three values that define a tile's presence over our height value range (0–255). This is the structure that I created:

```
struct STRN_TEXTURE_REGIONS
{
    int m_iLowHeight;       //lowest possible height (0%)
    int m_iOptimalHeight;   //optimal height (100%)
    int m_iHighHeight;      //highest possible height (0%)
};
```

An explanation of what each value does is best accomplished by checking out Figure 3.6.

For the explanation, we will make m_iLowHeight equivalent to 63 and m_iOptimalHeight equivalent to 128. Calculating the value for m_iHighHeight requires some simple math. We want to subtract m_iLowHeight from m_iOptimalHeight. Then we want to add m_iOptimalHeight to the result of the previous operation. We have our boundaries set (low: 63, optimal: 128, high: 193), so substitute those boundary values in Figure 3.6. Now imagine that we are trying to figure out how much presence the current tile has at a height of, say, 150. Imagine where that value would be on the line in Figure 3.6, taking into account the boundaries that we created. To save you the trouble of trying to figure it out, check out Figure 3.7.

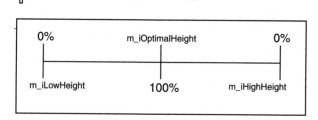

Figure 3.6 A "texture-presence" line.

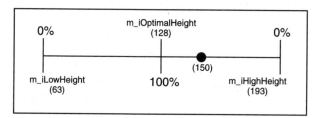

Figure 3.7 Applying the "texture-presence" line.

As you can see by the image, the texture's presence at that height (150) is about 70 percent. Now that we know that much information, what do we do with it? Well, we extract the RGB triplet from the texture's image and multiply it by 0.7f. The result is how much of the texture we want at our current pixel.

We need to create a function that will calculate the region percentage for us. This function is rather simple. It requires two trivial tests to see whether the given height is actually in the boundaries for the region; if it is not, exit the function. Next, we need to figure out where the height is located in the region. Is it below the optimal value, above it, or equivalent to the optimal value? The trivial case is if the height is equivalent to the optimal value; if it is, then the current tile has a texture presence of 100 percent at the current pixel, and we don't need to worry about interpolation at all.

If the height is below the optimal value, we need to reduce the given values to a simple fraction. To do this, we take the given height and subtract it by the low boundary for the region. Then we take the optimal boundary value and subtract it by the low boundary. We then divide the result from the first calculation by the result from the second calculation, and BAM! We have our presence percentage!

Here is the code for what was just discussed:

```
//height is below the optimal height
if( ucHeight<m_tiles.m_regions[tileType].m_iOptimalHeight )
{
    //calculate the texture percentage for the given tile's region
    fTemp1= ( float )m_tiles.m_regions[tileType].m_iLowHeight-
                      ucHeight;
    fTemp2= ( float )m_tiles.m_regions[tileType].m_iOptimalHeight-
                      m_tiles.m_regions[tileType].m_iLowHeight;

    return ( fTemp1/fTemp2 );
}
```

The final case is if the given height is above the optimal boundary. The calculations for this case are a bit more complex than when the height is below the boundary, but they still are not very hard. This explanation is *much* easier to see in its code form than it is in text, so here is the code:

```
//height is above the optimal height
else if( ucHeight>m_tiles.m_regions[tileType].m_iOptimalHeight )
{
    //calculate the texture percentage for the given tile's region
    fTemp1= ( float )m_tiles.m_regions[tileType].m_iHighHeight-
                      m_tiles.m_regions[tileType].m_iOptimalHeight;

    return ( ( fTemp1-( ucHeight-
        m_tiles.m_regions[tileType].m_iOptimalHeight ) )/fTemp1 );
}
```

The calculations, in theory, are basically the same that they were for the lower-than-optimal-height case, except that we had to be able to get the values down to a fraction that would make sense because 100 percent is lower than the height, instead of higher than the height. That's it!

The Tile System

Okay, now you know how to get the texture presence for *one* texture tile and *one* texture pixel. Now you need to apply everything you just learned to take all *four* texture tiles into account and create an entire texture map. This is a lot easier than it sounds, though, so don't get overwhelmed!

First, we need to create a texture tile structure that can manage all of our texture tiles. We do not need much information for each tile; all we need is a place to load the texture into and a region structure for each tile. We will also want to keep track of the total number of tiles that are loaded. With all of those requirements in mind, I created the STRN_TEXTURE_TILES structure, which looks like this:

```
struct STRN_TEXTURE_TILES
{
    STRN_TEXTURE_REGIONS m_regions[TRN_NUM_TILES];//texture regions
    CIMAGE textureTiles[TRN_NUM_TILES];              //texture tiles
    int iNumTiles;
};
```

Next, you need some texture tile management functions. I have functions for loading and unloading a single tile, along with a function that unloads all tiles at once. These functions are trivial to implement, so I won't show a snippet of them here. Just look in the code if you're interested. Other than that, you are ready to code the texture generation function!

To start the generation function, we need to figure out how many tiles are actually loaded. (We want the user to be able to generate a texture without all four tiles loaded.) After that is done, we need to reloop through the tiles to figure out the region boundaries for each tile. (We want the tile regions to be spaced out evenly across the 0–255 range). Here is how I went about doing this:

```
iLastHeight= -1;
for( i=0; i<TRN_NUM_TILES; i++ )
{
    //we only want to perform these calculations if we
    //actually have a tile loaded
    if( m_tiles.textureTiles[i].IsLoaded( ) )
    {
        //calculate the three height boundaries
        m_tiles.m_regions[i].m_iLowHeight= iLastHeight+1;
        iLastHeight+= 255/m_tiles.iNumTiles;
```

```
m_tiles.m_regions[i].m_iOptimalHeight= iLastHeight;

m_tiles.m_regions[i].m_iHighHeight= ( iLastHeight-
    m_tiles.m_regions[i].m_iLowHeight )+iLastHeight;
    }
}
```

The only thing that should look remotely odd here is the last segment
where we calculate m_iHighHeight, and even that should not look that
odd because we explained it earlier. (If it does look odd, refer back to
the beginning of this section where I explain the region boundaries.)

Creating the Texture Data

Now it is time to create the actual texture data. To do this, we need to
create three different for loops: one for the Z axis of the texture map,
one for the X axis, and one that goes through each tile. (This will be
the third tile loop in this function.) We also need to create three variables that will keep a running total of the current red, green, and blue
components for each pixel that we are calculating. This is what the
beginning of the actual texture generation should look like:

```
for( z=0; z<uiSize; z++ )
{
    for( x=0; x<uiSize; x++ )
    {
        //set our total color counters to 0.0f
        fTotalRed   = 0.0f;
        fTotalGreen= 0.0f;
        fTotalBlue = 0.0f;

        //loop through the tiles
        //for the third time in this function
        for( i=0; i<TRN_NUM_TILES; i++ )
        {
            //if the tile is loaded, we can perform the calculations
            if( m_tiles.textureTiles[i].IsLoaded( ) )
            {
```

Next, we need to extract the RGB values from the texture (at the
current pixel) into our temporary RGB unsigned char variables. Once
that is done, we need to figure out the current tile's presence at the

current pixel (using the function that we created earlier), multiply the temporary RGB variables by the result, and add that to our total RGB counters. Now we need to put the previous explanation into code:

```
//get the current color in the texture at the coordinates that we
//got in GetTexCoords
m_tiles.textureTiles[i].GetColor( uiTexX, uiTexZ,
                                  &ucRed, &ucGreen, &ucBlue );


//get the current coordinate's blending percentage for this tile
fBlend[i]=RegionPercent( i, InterpolateHeight( x, z, fMapRatio ) );


//calculate the RGB values that will be used
fTotalRed   += ucRed*fBlend[i];
fTotalGreen += ucGreen*fBlend[i];
fTotalBlue  += ucBlue*fBlend[i];
```

After we have looped through all four tiles, we then set the color for the pixel in the texture that we are creating, and then redo the whole thing for the next pixel. When we have completely finished generating the color values for the texture, we create the texture for use with our graphics API, and we're set!

Improving the Texture Generator

Okay, I lied. We are not all set. Our texture generation function has a couple of problems in its current form. These problems are as follows:

- We can only create a texture with a resolution of, or below, our heightmap.
- If we fix that problem, then we can only create a texture with a resolution of, or below, that of the smallest of our texture tiles.

Both of these problems are relatively easy to fix, however. Let's start with the heightmap resolution problem.

Getting Rid of the Heightmap Resolution Dependency

We need to let the user choose any texture size that he wants. (Well, almost any size. We want the dimensions to be a power of 2.) Early in our texture generation function, before we enter the huge series of for loops, we need to figure out the heightmap to texture map pixel ratio, which can be done like this:

```
fMapRatio= ( float )m_iSize/uiSize;
```

We then need to create a function that will interpolate the values that we extract from the heightmap. We will divide this interpolation function into two parts: one for the X axis and one for the Z axis. We will then get the average of the results for both parts, which is the value for our interpolated height value. This might not be the best way to go about things, but it works, and it works fast!

For this function, we need three arguments. The first two arguments are the unscaled (x, z) coordinate that we are getting information for. This will be rather high, and most likely, beyond the range of the heightmap. The third argument is the variable that has our calculate height to texture map pixel ratio (fMapRatio). Inside the function, we will scale the given (x, z) coordinates by the ratio variable and will use those for most of the function. To calculate the interpolation along the X axis, we will do this:

```
//set the middle boundary
ucLow= GetTrueHeightAtPoint( ( int )fScaledX, ( int )fScaledZ );

//set the high boundary
if( ( fScaledX+1 )>m_iSize )
    return ucLow;
else
    ucHighX= GetTrueHeightAtPoint( ( int )fScaledX+1,
                                   ( int )fScaledZ );

//calculate the interpolation (for the X axis)
fInterpolation= ( fScaledX-( int )fScaledX );
ucX            = ( ( ucHighX-ucLow )*fInterpolation )+ucLow;
```

As you can see, the first thing that we do is get the low height. Then we check to see if the next height on the heightmap is even on the heightmap. If it's not, then we have to be content with the low value. If the next height is on the heightmap, then we can get it and get ready to interpolate the two values. We get the difference between the floating-point scaled x value and the unsigned char scaled x value.

(It will have a lower degree of accuracy, which will define the amount of interpolation that we will use.) In the next calculation, we calculate the interpolation along the X axis. We then do the same thing for the Z axis, add the results from both calculations, and divide it by 2. That's all there is to it!

Getting Rid of the Tile Resolution Dependency

Okay, we're almost there. We have just one more thing to figure out, and that is how we can eliminate the tile-size boundary that is set upon the user. The solution is so obvious that you might wonder, "Why didn't I think of that?" Well, trust me, it took me a *long* time to figure out the solution, so don't feel bad. All we need to do is repeat the tile! I created a simple function that will give us the "new" texture coordinates that will repeat our texture for us. Here is the function:

```
void CTERRAIN::GetTexCoords( CIMAGE texture,
                                  unsigned int* x, unsigned int* y )
{
    unsigned int uiWidth = texture.GetWidth( );
    unsigned int uiHeight= texture.GetHeight( );
    int iRepeatX= -1;
    int iRepeatY= -1;
    int i= 0;

    //loop until we figure out how many times the tile
    //has repeated (on the X axis)
    while( iRepeatX==-1 )
    {
        i++;

        //if x is less than the total width,
        //then we found a winner!
        if( *x<( uiWidth*i ) )
            iRepeatX= i-1;
    }

    //prepare to figure out the repetition on the Y axis
    i= 0;
```

```
//loop until we figure out how many times the tile has repeated
//(on the Y axis)
while( iRepeatY==-1 )
{
    i++;

    //if y is less than the total height, then we have a bingo!
    if( *y<( uiHeight*i ) )
        iRepeatY= i-1;
}


//update the given texture coordinates
*x= *x-( uiWidth*iRepeatX );
*y= *y-( uiHeight*iRepeatY );
}
```

Most of this function consists of two while loops whose main goal is just trying to figure out how many times the texture has repeated before it reaches the coordinates that were given as arguments. After that is figured out, we are just scaling down the given coordinates so that they are back within the texture's value-range. (We don't want to try to extract information that is completely out of the texture's range. That would cause an error, and errors are bad.)

That's it! Our texture generation function is now complete! Check out Figure 3.8. In the demo, you'll notice a new field in the menu called Texture Map. In this field, you can generate a new texture of a higher resolution or save the current texture to the demo's directory. Speaking of a demo, you can see all of your hard work in demo3_2 on the CD in Code\Chapter 3\demo3_2. Just open up the workspace for the demo in Microsoft Visual C++ and start having some fun!

Using Detail Maps

1024 × 1024 is a rather large amount of data to achieve the amount of detail that we'd like to have in our texture. There must be another way to achieve our desired detail without wasting resources. Well, think no more! A cool way to add even more detail to your landscape is by using a *detail map*. A detail map is a grayscale texture like the one in Figure 3.9 that is repeated many times over a landscape and adds cool nuances, such as cracks, bumps, rocks, and other fun things.

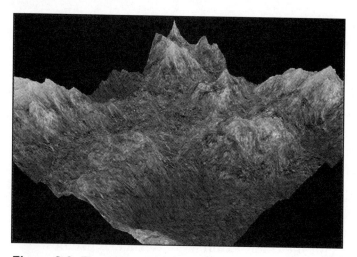

Figure 3.8 *The texture used in this screenshot from demo3_2 has a resolution of 1024 × 1024.*

Figure 3.9 *An example of a detail map.*

Adding detail map-support to your terrain engine is a simple process. Add some management functions for loading/unloading a detail map, a function that allows the user to decide how many times he wants the map to repeat across the landscape, and then all you have to do is edit your rendering code a bit. The hardest decision is deciding

whether to hardware multitexturing or just make two separate rendering passes. Because terrain meshes can become rather large, your best
bet is to stick to hardware multitexturing. Implementing hardware
multitexturing is beyond the scope of this book, but if you don't know
how to do it with your graphical API, it's a simple thing to implement,
and you should learn it. In case you don't know a good place to learn
an API, check out *OpenGL Game Programming* (Astle/Hawkins) or
Special Effects Game Programming with DirectX 8.0 (McCuskey), both
published by Premier Press—a great publisher if I do so say myself!

To edit your rendering code, just set the base color texture (the one
we generated earlier, for instance) to the first texture unit, and then
set your detail texture to the second texture unit. Remember how the
texture coordinates for the color texture were calculated like this?

```
fTexLeft  = ( float )x/m_iSize;
fTexBottom= ( float )z/m_iSize;
fTexTop   = ( float )( z+1 )/m_iSize;
```

Well, we just have to make a slight modification to those calculations
to get the texture coordinates for our detail texture:

```
fTexLeft  = ( float )( x/m_iSize )*m_iRepeatDetailMap );
fTexBottom= ( float )( z/m_iSize )*m_iRepeatDetailMap );
fTexTop   = ( float )( ( z+1 )/m_iSize )*m_iRepeatDetailMap );
```

`m_iRepeatDetailMap` is how many times the user wants the detail map to
repeat across the landscape. The hardest part of detail mapping is setting up multitexturing with your graphics API, but if you're using
OpenGL, I set everything up for you. (Yeah, I know I'm a nice guy,
and my birthday is on March 11 if you feel the need to repay me!) To
see the effect that a detail map can have on your terrain, look at the
difference between a terrain that uses a 256×256 procedural texture
without a detail map (the left side of Figure 3.10) and terrain that uses
the same 256×256 texture, except *with* a detail map (the right side of
Figure 3.10).

See how much more detail the image on the right has? The best part
is that adding that extensive amount of detail is simple. Check out
demo3_3 on the CD in Code\Chapter 3\demo3_3, which shows the
new detail map code in action. The only changed controls from the
rest of the demos are that T turns off detail mapping and D turns
detail mapping back on. (Detail mapping is on by default.)

Figure 3.10 *Comparison of two terrain images, one without a detail map (left) and one with a detail map (right).*

Summary

We learned a lot about texturing terrain in this chapter. We started off with simple texturing (stretching a single texture across an entire landscape), and then we kicked things into high gear with procedural texture generation. We ended with a simple but cool technique called detail mapping. In the next chapter, we will learn the next step in making our terrain more realistic: lighting. If you happen to like texturing techniques, you might want to check out Tobias Franke's article titled "Terrain Texture Generation"[1] or Yordan Gyurchev's article titled "Generating Terrain Textures."[2] You also might be interested in Jeff Lander's article titled "Terrain Texturing,"[3] which presents a dynamic texture tiling solution.

References

1 Franke, Tobias. "Terrain Texture Generation." 2001. http://www.flipcode.com/tutorials/tut_proctext.shtml.

2 Gyurchev, Yordan. "Generating Terrain Textures." 2001. http://www.flipcode.com/tutorials/tut_terrtex.shtml.

3 Lander, Jeff. "Terrain Texturing." Delphi3D-Rapid OpenGL Development. 2002. http://www.delphi3d.net/articles/viewarticle.php?article=terraintex.htm.

CHAPTER 4

LIGHTING TERRAIN

Texturing terrain brought about a new level of detail into our terrain, and lighting terrain will bring a whole new level of realism. The question is this: How do we light our terrain as quickly as possible while still keeping a high level of realism? Well, all the techniques that I will be teaching you are all fast (if rough) ways of lighting terrain. I will not be going into complicated global illumination algorithms (although I will point you to some places where you can get information on some of them) because realistic terrain lighting can probably cover an entire book on its own. With that said, this is the agenda for this chapter:

- Height-based lighting
- Hardware lighting
- Applying a lightmap to terrain
- The ultra-cool slope-lighting algorithm

I'll keep this discussion of lighting decently short because I know that you (or if you don't, then I know I do) want to get started with the cool terrain algorithms that I'll be presenting in the next three chapters. Let's get going!

Height-Based Lighting

Height-based lighting is simple and unrealistic, but it *is* a type of lighting, so I figured I'd at least cover it briefly. We used height-based lighting in all of the demos in Chapter 2, "Terrain 101," so you have used it before even if you didn't know it.

Height-based lighting is just that—lighting based off the height of a vertex. High vertices (based on height data from the terrain patch's height data) are brighter than low vertices, and that's all there is to it. All that we need to do is use our GetTrueHeightAtPoint function (member of the CTERRAIN class) to extract the brightness of the pixel at the current (x, z) location (the value will be in the range of 0–255) from the heightmap, and that is our brightness value. It's that simple! Figure 4.1 reinforces the concept.

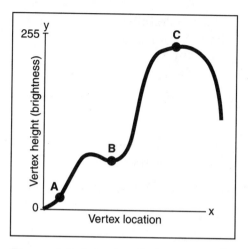

Figure 4.1 *A visual explanation of height-based lighting.*

In the figure, vertex A would be almost black, vertex B would be a bit brighter, and vertex C would be completely illuminated (white). There you go—an entire explanation of height-based lighting in three paragraphs and one figure!

Now you know what height-based lighting is, but how do you calculate the lighting values inside your code? Well, it is rather simple, considering that you have a heightmap loaded. For example, say you are trying to calculate the brightness for vertex (157, 227) in your terrain. Well, the vertex's brightness would simply be the height value that you extract from the heightmap.

```
ucShade= GetTrueHeightAtPoint( 157, 227 );
```

ucShade is the variable that we store our lighting value in, and GetTrueHeightAtPoint extracts information from our heightmap, at vertex (157, 227) in this case, in a range of 0 (dark) to 255 (bright). Now, let's add some color to our lighting!

Coloring the Light Source

We do not always want our lighting color to be grayscale (black to white). Most of the time, we would like our lighting to be colored for various situations. For instance, if it were a cloudless evening, the user would be experiencing a nice sunset, so we'd want our lighting color to be a shade of orange, pink, or purple. We need to create a vector for our lighting color information and a simple function that will set the color of the light. (We want the lighting values to be in the range of 0.0f–1.0f. You'll find out why in a second.) After we have that done, we can take the lighting value that we retrieved earlier and multiply that by each value in the RGB light color vector using this equation:

```
Intensity= shade*color
```

Now, using that equation, we can apply it to figure out the RGB color components, and then send them to the rendering API:

```
ColorToAPI( ( unsigned char )( ucShade*m_vecLightColor[0] ),
            ( unsigned char )( ucShade*m_vecLightColor[1] ),
            ( unsigned char )( ucShade*m_vecLightColor[2] ) );
```

ucShade is the brightness value that we calculated earlier, and vecLightColor is the color of our light. Now check out demo4_1 (on the CD under Code\Chapter 4\demo4_1) and Figure 4.2. If you need a refresher on the demo's controls, check out Table 4.1.

When you look at the figure, you notice that the lower areas of the terrain are rather dark and that the high areas of the terrain are bright. This is exactly what height-based lighting does: High areas are bright, and low areas are dark. What's the problem with this algorithm? First, it is incredibly unrealistic. This algorithm doesn't take into account

Figure 4.2 *A screenshot from demo4_1.*

Table 4.1 Controls for demo 4_1

Key	Function
Escape / Q	Quit the program
Up arrow	Move forward
Down arrow	Move backward
Right arrow	Strafe right
Left arrow	Strafe left
T	Toggle texture mapping
D	Toggle detail mapping
W	Render in wireframe mode
S	Render in solid/fill mode
+ / -	Increase/decrease mouse sensitivity
] / [	Increase/decrease movement sensitivity

that it is possible for the sun to be shining directly at a "dip" in the terrain (a low height area), which would make that area very bright. This problem is shown in Figure 4.3.

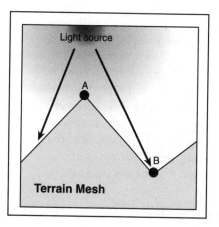

Figure 4.3 *One problem with height-based lighting.*

You see, in Figure 4.3, the sun reaches both vertices A and B, but according to the way we would be lighting the terrain with the height-based lighting technique, vertex A would be bright and vertex B would be dark, which is incorrect (as the figure shows).

The second problem with this technique is that it provides you with very little freedom over the way you want your terrain's lighting to look. Now we need to proceed and discuss more versatile and realistic ways of lighting terrain.

Hardware Lighting

This technique has two major problems. First, it is highly API dependent, so I won't be showing you code or giving you a demo of it. Second, it is pretty useless for dynamic terrain meshes—the kind that we will be working with for the next three chapters. Because of these issues, I'll just give you some basic implementation details here.

Hardware lighting requires you to calculate the surface normal for every triangle that you render. The best time to do this is in the pre-processing segment of your demo; that way, the calculations do not bog down the program. After you calculate the normal, you just send it to the API for the current triangle that you want to render, and you're done.

CAUTION

Be sure that you have hardware lighting set up correctly with your API before you do anything. Hardware lighting can be, at times, a real pain to set up, so don't be too surprised if your terrain isn't lit or is lit incorrectly the first time you try to implement it. You need to make sure that you have a customized light source (with the correct attenuation, diffuse/specular/ambient values, and so on). After you have your light set up, be sure that you enabled the light source and the lighting component of your API in general. Many people come to me with questions about hardware lighting, and 75 percent of them have forgotten to enable their light source! Don't be a statistic.

This technique works great for static terrain meshes like the kind that we have been using in the past two chapters and the one we are using in this chapter. It makes dynamic lighting and day/night simulations a breeze. However, because hardware lighting is mostly vertex based, dynamic terrain meshes do not look good being hardware lit. (Dynamic meshes have constantly shifting vertices.) That's it for our discussion of hardware lighting. Hope you didn't blink.

Lightmapping

We will use lightmapping constantly throughout this book. A *lightmap* is exactly like a heightmap (discussed in Chapter 2), except that instead of having information for heights, the lightmap contains only lighting information. All of the code for loading, saving, and unloading a lightmap is the same as that of the corresponding procedures for heightmaps (except that the lightmap manipulation functions deal with different variables than the heightmap functions), so I won't waste your valuable time by going through each function again. Our lightmap information is going to be stored in a grayscale RAW texture, just like our heightmaps, except the information in the lightmap *only* pertains to lighting. For instance, look at the heightmap and the lightmap in Figure 4.4, and then look at the result that is achieved in Figure 4.5. See how a lightmap affects the terrain lighting?

See how the light in Figure 4.5 is in a spherical shape exactly like the lightmap in Figure 4.4? That is why we use lightmaps: to define the exact type of lighting that we want for a patch of terrain. And because you can pre-create lightmaps, you can use various algorithms to generate them. You can generate lightmaps in many ways. Some of these ways are

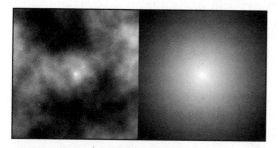

Figure 4.4 *The heightmap (left) and the lightmap (right) for the terrain in Figure 4.5.*

Figure 4.5 *The terrain created from the heightmap and lightmap in Figure 4.4.*

complicated—but good looking—global illumination techniques. I will be showing you one such way to create a lightmap in the next section.

After you have a lightmap loaded in the same fashion that we loaded the heightmap, you need to create a function that will extract the brightness at a given pixel:

```
inline unsigned char GetBrightnessAtPoint( int x, int z )
{   return ( m_lightmap.m_ucpData[( z*m_lightmap.m_iSize )+x] );   }
```

Remember how we used GetTrueHeightAtPoint to get the brightness information for height-based lighting in demo4_2? All we have to do is replace that call with a call to GetBrightnessAtPoint and we're set! See how easy all of these lighting techniques are? Check out demo4_2 on the CD under Code\Chapter 4\demo4_2, and try creating some of your own little heightmaps and seeing how they turn out. I created an interesting little lightmap in Figure 4.6, with the result shown in Figure 4.7.

As if it weren't obvious before, I am suffering from an extreme combination of having too much time on my hands and having far too much fun with this book!

Lightmapping is of such critical importance in games that I feel the urge to expand on some of its more advanced features. I covered everything that you need to do to "paste" a lightmap onto terrain, but the more advanced lightmapping concepts concentrate on the generation of a lightmap. (I'll be showing you one such algorithm a bit later.)

Figure 4.6 *The lightmap used to create the terrain in Figure 4.7.*

Figure 4.7 *The terrain created from the lightmap in Figure 4.6.*

Many games, such as *Max-Payne* and *Quake 2*, use a method known as radiosity. (Visit http://freespace.virgin.net/hugo.elias/radiosity/ radiosity.htm if you would like an explanation of the technique.) Notice that the games I mentioned are both indoor-based games, and terrain is an outdoor topic, which, as you might guess, means that we have to find another technique to calculate our lightmaps. Luckily for us, many different techniques are available (almost a bewildering amount, in fact). I will be providing one such simple algorithm, but let it be known that it *is* a simple algorithm, and not nearly as powerful as some of the other global illumination techniques in existence, one of which I will refer to at the end of this chapter.

Slope Lighting

Let me get this out of my system right now: This is one of the coolest algorithms that I've come across in a long time. It is incredibly simple to use, and it provides sharp-looking results. *Slope lighting*[1] is a simple lighting technique that shades vertices according to their height in relation to a nearby vertex.

Okay, Slope Lighting Is Cool, But How Is It Performed?

To slope light terrain, we are going to retrieve the height from the vertex next to the current vertex (the direction will be dictated by the light's direction), and then subtract it by the current vertex's height. Basically, we are checking to see if the other vertex is going to be casting a shadow upon the current vertex. I think this is the perfect time for a real-life example. Say you were standing in front of a large building that was blocking the sun from your point of view. The building would be casting a shadow over you, as in Figure 4.8.

As you can see in the figure, the light source's rays will not reach your position due to the large building obstructing them. The end result is that you will be standing in a shadowy area, making you appear darker to the people who are receiving the light's rays. This is the same concept we are trying to achieve in slope lighting—shading vertices that

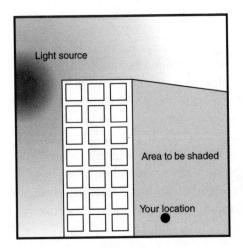

Figure 4.8 *The building analogy.*

are having a light source's rays blocked by the higher vertex before them. This concept is further explained in Figure 4.9.

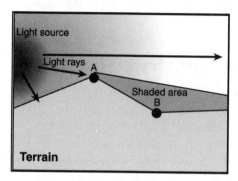

Figure 4.9 *A visual example of slope lighting.*

As you can see in the figure, the light source sends out all kinds of light rays (a near infinite amount, actually) but, in this case, none of them will reach vertex B because vertex A is blocking the light. Just because vertex B receives no direct light rays does not mean it is completely dark; some of the light that the other vertices receive "bleeds" out into the vertex, slightly illuminating it. A vertex is never completely dark.

There is a slight flaw in this algorithm, and that is when you set the light's direction, it must be in increments of 45 degrees. For instance, the left side of Figure 4.10 is lit by a light with a direction of (1, 1). If we wanted to move the light to the left, we would have to change the light to a direction of (0, 1), which would cause the light to move 45 degree to the left instead of a smooth transition like a light movement of 2–5 degrees at a time.

Figure 4.10 *Terrain that is slope-lit with a light direction of (1, 1) (left) and a light direction of (0, 1) (right).*

Now, if you'll notice, there really is not a huge difference between these images. Therefore, you can easily get away with changing the light's direction in real-time. Most users won't notice the slight "jump" in shading.

Creating a Slope-Lighting System

We need to add a few variables to our CTERRAIN class before we can start writing the slope-lighting code. (If you think this class is getting filled with a lot of extra features *now*, just wait until *later*!) We need to be able to define the minimum/maximum brightness for our terrain because, as I said earlier, rarely is a shadowed vertex ever *completely* darkened. We also need variables for the light's softness and the light's direction, both of which need to be used if we want to achieve realistic results. In addition, we want a function that will easily let users customize the slope lighting system's parameters:

```
inline void CustomizeSlopeLighting( int iDirX, int iDirZ,
                                    float fMinBrightness,
                                    float fMaxBrightness,
                                    float fSoftness )
{
    //set the light direction
    m_iDirectionX= iDirX;
    m_iDirectionZ= iDirZ;

    //set the minimum/maximum shading values
    m_fMinBrightness= fMinBrightness;
    m_fMaxBrightness= fMaxBrightness;

    //set the light's softness
    m_fLightSoftness= fSoftness;
}
```

Dynamically Creating Lightmaps

Before we go any further, do you recall me saying that the most critical lightmapping algorithms consist of lightmap generation? Well, now we are going to create a function that will generate a lightmap for use by our terrain. You can choose to calculate the lighting every frame (it is not that slow of a process with the algorithms that I am presenting here), but it is much better to calculate once at the beginning of a demo and then calculate the lighting again whenever it is needed. Here is the first half of the function that I created to do this:

```
void CTERRAIN::CalculateLighting( void )
{
    float fShade;
    int x, z;

    //a lightmap has already been provided, no need to create one
    if( m_lightingType==LIGHTMAP )
            return;

    //allocate memory if it is needed
    if( m_lightmap.m_iSize!=m_iSize || m_lightmap.m_ucpData==NULL )
    {
        //delete the memory for the old data
        delete[] m_lightmap.m_ucpData;

        //allocate memory for the new lightmap data buffer
        m_lightmap.m_ucpData= new unsigned char [m_iSize*m_iSize];
        m_lightmap.m_iSize= m_iSize;
    }

    //loop through all vertices
    for( z=0; z<m_iSize; z++ )
    {
        for( x=0; x<m_iSize; x++ )
        {
            //using height-based lighting, trivial
            if( m_lightingType==HEIGHT_BASED )
                SetBrightnessAtPoint( x, z,
                                            GetTrueHeightAtPoint( x, z ) );
```

Up to this point, you should be able to comprehend everything. We start out by checking to see whether the user is using a premade lightmap. If he is, then we don't want to overwrite the information in the lightmap. Then we need to see whether we need to allocate memory for the lightmap. After that, we start our loop through all of the vertices—the lightmap needs to be the same size as our heightmap—and check to see whether the user is using height-based lighting. If he is, then we set the current pixel to the same pixel that is in the heightmap. The remainder of the function has to do with slope lighting, so I'll describe it in two sections:

```
//using the slope-lighting technique
else if( m_lightingType==SLOPE_LIGHT )
{
    //ensure that we won't be stepping over array boundaries by
    //doing this
    if( z>=m_iDirectionZ && x>=m_iDirectionX )
    {
        //calculate the shading value using the "slope lighting"
        //algorithm
        fShade= 1.0f-( GetTrueHeightAtPoint( x-m_iDirectionX,
                                             z-m_iDirectionZ ) -
            GetTrueHeightAtPoint( x, z ) )/m_fLightSoftness;
    }
```

This is where the bulk of the slope-lighting calculations take place. As you can see, we subtract the height of the vertex before the current one—in the direction that the user specifies—by the current vertex. We are trying to see how much of a shadow the previous vertex casts. We then divide that value by the light softness and subtract 1.0f from the value that we have after the division. I really haven't talked about how the light's softness affects things, so check out Figure 4.11, where I took a screenshot using three different levels of softness.

And now, the rest of the function:

```
        //if we are stepping over a boundary, then just
        //return a very bright color value (white)
        else
            fShade= 1.0f;

        //clamp the shading value to the minimum/maximum
        //brightness boundaries
        if( fShade<m_fMinBrightness )
            fShade= m_fMinBrightness;
        if( fShade>m_fMaxBrightness )
            fShade= m_fMaxBrightness;
```

```
//set the new brightness for our lightmap
SetBrightnessAtPoint( x, z,
                        ( unsigned char )( fShade*255 ) );
                }
            }
        }
}
```

In this section, we clamp fShade to the minimum/maximum brightness boundaries and then set the brightness at the current point in the lightmap. In demo4_3 (on the CD under Code\Chapter 4\demo4_3), I added a cool new dialog box (see Figure 4.12) that lets you fully customize the slope-lighting system dynamically. Have some fun with it!

Figure 4.11 *Varying levels of light softness: a value of 1 (left), 10 (center), and 15 (right).*

Customize Slope Lighting ✕

Color (R, G, B values in the range of 0-255)
Red: 255 Green: 255 Blue: 255

Light Direction: X: 1   Z: 1

Brightness (in the range of 0-255):
Min: 51   Max: 229

Light Softness: 15

OK

Cancel

Figure 4.12 *The Customize Slope Lighting dialog box in demo4_3.*

Summary

This chapter has been a quick run-through of some simple lighting
techniques that can add a new level of realism to your terrain. We
talked about height-based lighting, hardware lighting, lightmapping,
and slope-lighting. Slope-lighting is probably your best bet for simple
terrain demos. I didn't have time to mention one really cool global
illumination technique, which is Hoffman and Mitchell's article
"Real-Time Photorealistic Terrain Lighting," but if you're interested
in terrain lighting, it is definitely worth a look. Anyway, you'd better
prepare yourself—you're about to enter the hardcore terrain
programming section, which contains all sorts of information on
advanced terrain algorithms.

References

1 Van Noland, Charlie. "Slope Lighting Terrain." 2002.
http://www.gamedev.net/reference/articles/article1436.asp.

PART TWO

Advanced Terrain Programming

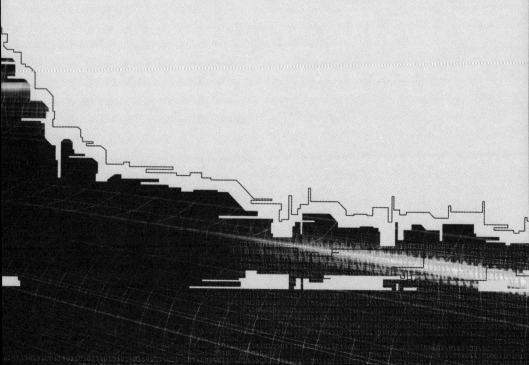

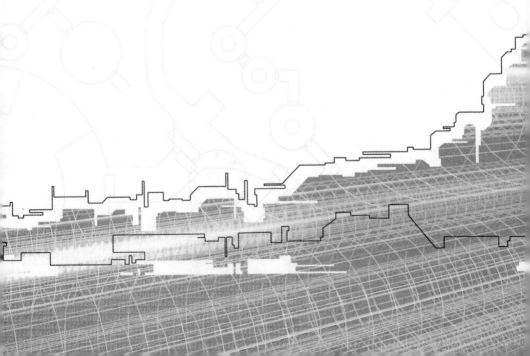

CHAPTER 5

GEOMIP-MAPPING FOR THE CLOD IMPAIRED

Woohoo! You are now going to learn all about hardcore terrain programming, which consists of incredibly difficult algorithms. Actually, that's a lie. The three algorithms I'm going to explain in this chapter were chosen because of their simplicity and efficiency. And, for once in this book, I'm going to spare you from a long drawn-out introduction and simply tell you the agenda for this chapter:

- An explanation of what Continuous Level of Detail means
- The theory behind geomipmapping
- The method for implementing geomipmapping

For simplicity, I broke the agenda into three parts. Despite this breakdown, this chapter is rather large. Don't let the size of this chapter intimidate you, however; the content will be presented, as always, in a fun and simple manner. Note that I am changing the style of learning a bit, though. Chapters 5, 6, and 7 focus more on algorithmic explanations and pseudo-code than the earlier chapters do. In these later chapters, I still provide you with demos and implementations of my own, but the implementations are simple, and you should use them only in conjunction with the text. With that said, let's get started.

CLOD Terrain 101

You've heard the term *Continuous Level of Detail* (CLOD) several times in this book, but it's about time that I tell you what it actually is. A CLOD algorithm, in one sentence, is a dynamic polygonal mesh that "gives" extra triangles to areas that require more detail. That's a simple statement, but you'll understand a lot more about CLOD by the end of this section, and you'll understand even more by the end of this chapter. Don't fret if you don't understand what CLOD is yet.

Why Bother with CLOD Terrain?

CLOD algorithms require more research, are harder to code, and take up more CPU cycles than your average brute force implementation.

With that in mind, why would you want to bother with a CLOD algorithm? It's simple really: to create a more realistic, more detailed and, most importantly, a faster patch of terrain.

More Detail Is Added
Where More Detail Is Needed

One of the basic ideas of CLOD is that we want to add more detail (more triangles) where it is needed. For instance, if we had a rather smooth patch of terrain (see Figure 5.1), we would want fewer triangles on average than we would for a more chaotic patch (see Figure 5.2).

Figure 5.1 *Few triangles would be needed to render this smooth patch of terrain.*

Figure 5.2 *Many triangles would be needed to render this chaotic patch of terrain.*

However, not all algorithms worry about the distribution of triangles to areas that require more detail. Geomipmapping doesn't distribute more triangles to areas that require more detail, but Rottger's Quadtree algorithm (in Chapter 6, "Climbing the Quadtree) does. Therefore, saying that CLOD, as a whole, adds more detail to areas that require it, is not always true, but for most cases, it is. Am I thoroughly confusing you yet?

Cull Like You've Never Culled Before!

Another positive to CLOD-based algorithms is that they allow more selective culling of polygons than brute force methods do. This means that polygons that aren't seen won't be sent to the API. For instance, the geomipmapping implementation that we are about to start work on uses a series of landscape patches. If a patch isn't visible, we eliminate a potential 289 rendered vertices (for a 17×17 vertex patch) in one fell swoop. This is a huge load off of the graphics card, and the culling isn't even CPU intensive. Using a simple method, we please both the GPU and the CPU, making your motherboard happier as a whole.

Not Everything Is Happy in the Land of CLOD Terrain

Using CLOD terrain algorithms does have some drawbacks, though. Oddly enough, the universe aided me in writing this section by placing the August issue of *Game Developer Magazine* in my mailbox earlier today. The main drawback in most CLOD algorithms is the "bookkeeping" involved in updating the polygonal mesh every frame. [1]

This "bookkeeping" drawback wasn't nearly as prevalent when most of these algorithms (geomipmapping, Rottger's quadtree algorithm, and ROAM) were designed. This is because the algorithms wanted to put most of the workload on the CPU and send as little information as necessary to the GPU. Since then, however, things have changed quite a bit. Now we want to put a larger focus on the GPU than the CPU.

Wrapping Up Your Introduction to CLOD Terrain

Obviously, if the geomipmapping, quadtree, and ROAM algorithms were out of date, you wouldn't be reading about them right now, which means that someone, somewhere (heck, maybe even me) came up with some optimizations for each algorithm that still make them important to modern-day terrain rendering. With that in mind, I'll quit babbling about CLOD and start babbling about implementing geomipmapping.

Geomipmapping Theory for the Semi-CLOD Impaired

Geomipmapping, developed by Willem H. de Boer, is a CLOD algorithm that is GPU friendly. It is also a simple algorithm that is perfect for your transition into the land of CLOD landscapes. As we go along, you might want to refer to the actual geomipmapping whitepaper, which I have placed on the accompanying CD-ROM for your convenience. (It's named Algorithm Whitepapers/geomipmapping.pdf.)

Simply the Basics

If you are familiar with the texturing concept of mipmapping, then geomipmapping should seem like familiar ground to you. The concepts are the same, except that instead of dealing with textures, we're dealing with vertices of a patch of terrain. The driving concept of geomipmapping is that you have a set patch of terrain. For this explanation, I'll say it's a patch with a size of 5 vertices (a 5 × 5 patch). That 5 × 5 patch is going to have several levels of detail, with level 0 being the most detailed and, in this case, level 2 being the least detailed. Look at Figure 5.3 if you need a visual explanation of what each patch looks like at its various levels. In the figure, black vertices are *not* sent to the rendering API, but the white ones are.

If you referred to the Willem de Boer's geomipmapping whitepaper, you might have noticed that the triangle arrangement shown in Figure 5.3 is slightly different from the arrangement shown in the whitepaper. The reason I did this will become clear to you a bit later, but for now, just know that I did it for a reason.

It's about time that we discussed geomipmapping a bit more. I gave you the basics earlier, but now it's time that you know *everything*...

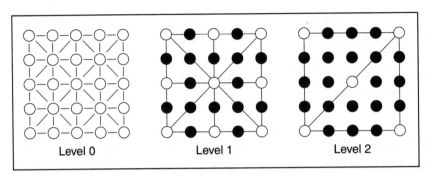

Figure 5.3 *Triangle arrangement for a patch of terrain, in which the most detailed arrangement is on the left, and the least detailed arrangement is on the right.*

Well, almost everything. I might withhold some information for your protection.

As I said earlier, geomipmapping is similar to texture mipmapping except that we're using land patches instead of texture patches. What we need to do, starting from the user's point in 3D space (the camera's eye position), is make all of the patches around the viewer be the most detailed because those patches are what the user sees the most of. At a certain distance away, we'll switch to a lower level of patch detail. And, at another distance away, we'll switch to an even lower level of detail. Figure 5.4 explains this visually.

As you can see in the figure, the patches in the immediate area of the viewer's position have a Level of Detail (LOD) of 0, which means that those patches are of the highest level of detail. As the patches become farther away, they change to a level of 1, which is the second highest level of detail. And even farther away from the viewer, the patches have a level of 2, which is the lowest level of detail presented in the image.

Triangle Arrangement Made Easy

Earlier, you might have noticed that the triangle arrangement I used in Figure 5.3 is quite different from the one presented in the geomipmapping paper I referred you to (on the CD or on the Internet at the URL presented at the end of this chapter). In case you don't have access to that paper right now, look at Figure 5.5 to see what the paper's suggested triangle arrangement looks like.

2	2	2	2	2	2	2	2
1	1	1	1	1	1	2	2
1	1	1	1	1	1	2	2
0	0	0	0	1	1	2	2
0	0	0	0	1	1	2	2
0	0	0	0	1	1	2	2
0	0	0	0	1	1	2	2
1	1	1	1	1	1	2	2

Eye Position

Figure 5.4 *In the geomipmapping algorithm, as a patch of terrain gets farther away from the viewer, it switches to a lower level of detail.*

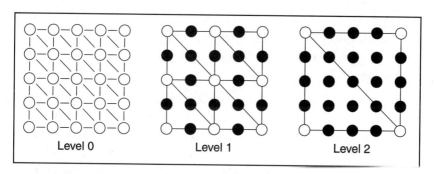

Figure 5.5 *The triangle arrangement for patch rendering presented in the geomipmapping whitepaper.*

This arrangement might seem like a better idea, and it is for the most part. (Warning: I'm going to get slightly sidetracked right here.) Triangle strips are definitely the way to go if you plan to use vertex buffers to render the patches, which is my suggestion to you. However, because implementing a vertex buffer rendering system is highly dependent on API, I chose to use immediate mode rendering because it is much easier to convert to another API's syntax if needed. Using a vertex buffer for rendering provides a huge speed increase for any terrain implementation because it reduces the function overhead that is present when you're sending each vertex, texture coordinate, color, and so on to the API individually. In addition, most graphics cards prefer vertex information being sent in the form of a vertex buffer. In the end, I recommend that you use vertex buffers for terrain rendering. You'll get a tremendous increase in speed, and that is *always* worth the extra effort it takes to achieve it. If you'd like to see an example of a geomipmapping-esque technique using Direct3D vertex buffers, look at "Simplified Terrain Using Interlocking Tiles," published in *Game Programming Gems*, volume 2.

Anyway, it's time to get back on topic. The arrangement shown in Figure 5.3 is the way we will render our patches. This arrangement provides us with one huge benefit: It allows us to easily skip rendering a vertex when we need to, which is quite often. That brings me to our next topic of discussion.

Hacks and Cracks, But Mostly Just Cracks

Often when you're dealing with CLOD terrain algorithms, you must deal with the subject of *cracking*. Cracking occurs, in the case of geomipmapping, when a highly detailed patch resides next to a lower detailed patch (see Figure 5.6).

As you can see from the figure, the patch on the left is of a higher level of detail than the patch on the right. Our problem lies at points A and B. The problem is that there is a higher level of detail on the left side of point A than there is on point B. This means that the left patch is rendering the exact height at point A, but the right patch is just getting the average of the height above it and the height below it.

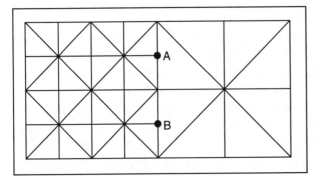

Figure 5.6 *Two patches, side by side, with different levels of detail.*

This whole "cracking" thing might not seem like such a big deal, but check out Figure 5.7, which shows a screenshot of my geomipmapping implementation without noncracking measures taken.

Figure 5.7 *A screenshot from a geomipmapping implementation, which does not implement anti-cracking measures.*

It's not exactly a smooth landscape, is it? Just look at all those gaping holes in the scenery. Let's fix it!

Crack-Proofing Your Geomipmapping Engine

Crack-proofing your geomipmapping engine is a lot easier than it might sound. You have the added benefit of having someone (that would be me) explain this concept to you, which makes the whole process as easy as... well, something easy.

We have two possible ways of fixing the cracking problem. One way is to add vertices to the patch with the lower amount of detail so that the vertices in question will be of the same height as the higher detailed patch's corresponding vertices. This solution could be ugly, though, and it means that we'd have to do some rearranging of the patch (add another triangle fan).

The other way of solving this problem is to omit vertices from the more detailed patch. This solves the cracking problem seamlessly and effortlessly. Check out Figure 5.8 to see how easy it is to simply omit a vertex and fix the crack.

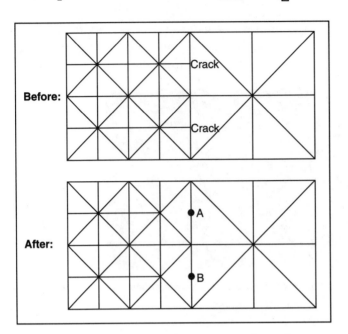

Figure 5.8 *Crack elimination by omitting rendering the vertex at points A and B.*

Where Art Thou Crack?

You know what causes cracks and how to fix them. The real question is this: How do you know *when* to fix them? Basically, when you're rendering the current patch, you need to test the patches around it (see Figure 5.9) to see whether they are of a lower detail level. If they are, you know you need to omit some vertices.

Testing each patch isn't difficult. You just need to implement a series of simple if-else statements. (Pseudo-code is shown next.)

```
If LeftPatch.LOD is less than CurrentPatch.LOD
    RenderLeftVertex= true;
Else
    RenderLeftVertex= false;

If RightPatch.LOD is less than CurrentPatch.LOD
    RenderRightVertex= true;
Else
```

```
        RenderRightVertex = false;

If UpperPatch.LOD is less than CurrentPatch.LOD
        RenderUpperVertex= true;
Else
        RenderUpperVertex= false;

If LowerPatch.LOD is less than CurrentPatch.LOD
        RenderLowerVertex= true;
Else
        RenderLowerVertex = false;
```

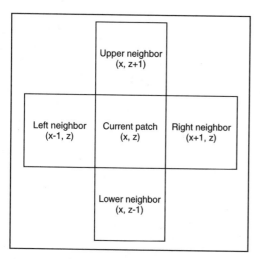

Figure 5.9 *The neighbor patches that need to be tested to see whether they have a lower LOD.*

See how simple it is? After the testing, while rendering your triangle fan, you skip the vertices in the direction of the coarser patch. For instance, if the right patch is of a coarser level of detail, and your current patch is of a high level of detail (multiple columns/rows of triangle fans are rendered), then you only want to skip the vertices on the far right of the patch (see Figure 5.10).

CAUTION

Be careful that you omit only the necessary vertices. Otherwise, you could end up with a patch full of vertices that you didn't mean to omit. For instance, in Figure 5.10, the patch consists of multiple columns and rows of triangle fans. You don't want to omit the right vertex for every fan; you just want to omit the right vertex for the fans in the right-most column.

And that is it for your simple geomipmapping theory! Now it's about time that we implemented everything we just learned.

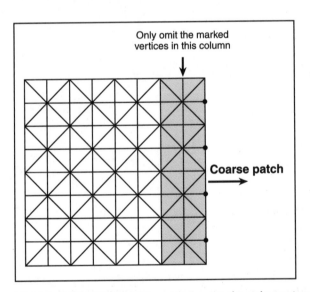

Figure 5.10 *A patch that needs to omit the right vertices in the fans in the right-most column to prevent cracking with the patch to the right.*

Implementing Geomipmapping for the Very Slightly CLOD Impaired

You know the theory behind the geomipmapping basics, but now we need to implement it. This should not tax your brain too much. The hard part is already over with, and as usual, we'll be taking one step at a time. Get some caffeine, lock your doors, and get some good music going!

Patch It Up

Because geomipmapping is composed of a series of patches, it is probably a good idea to start off the implementation by creating the patch data structure. The structure really does not need to contain much information, and the less we need to include, the better. In fact, this will be the smallest structure you will ever see created in this book. Don't get too accustomed to its nice size!

All the patch structure really needs is two variables. One variable will keep track of the patch's current level of detail, and one variable will store the distance from the center of the patch to the camera's position. That's all there is to it! That is the entire patch data structure. Here it is, in code:

```
struct SGEOMM_PATCH
{
        float m_fDistance;

        int   m_iLOD;
};
```

It might look like a tiny structure, but remember: Big things come in small packages. As small as that package is, we will be using it constantly, so make sure you spend hours memorizing its members.

Creating the Basic Geomipmapping Implementation

Yeah, no more of this wimpy two-member data structure stuff. Now we're going to start work on the workhorse of the geomipmapping engine—the geomipmapping class. To start, we need a pointer to hold our patch information, which will be dynamically allocated at some point in our demo. Next, we need to figure out the patch size (in vertices) and how many patches the terrain will have per side. The patch size is completely up to the user, so we can let him specify the patch size he likes when he initializes the class. (I tend to stick with a patch size of about 17×17 vertices because it provides a nice mix of detail and speed. This chapter's explanations assume a patch of that size.)

> **CAUTION**
>
> The geomipmapping implementation is based on a $2^N + 1$ pixel square height map. This means that you can't use the midpoint displacement fractal height map generator to generate heightmaps. Stick with the fault formation generator for all of your heightmaps.

Geomipmapping Initialization

For initialization of the geomipmapping system, all we need from the user is the patch size he desires. (I'll reinstate my suggestion of 17×17 vertices.) After we have that, we can initialize the system.

First we need to calculate how many patches will be on each side of the terrain. We figure this by taking the size of the height map and dividing it by the size of an individual patch, as shown in Figure 5.11.

P represents the number of patches per side, h represents the size of the heightmap, and s represents the size of an individual patch. With that equation in mind, peek ahead to Figure 5.12 to see what variables we are going to plug into the equation a bit later.

After we calculate the number of patches per side, we need to allocate the terrain patch buffer by squaring the number of patches per side. (This is the value that we just finished calculating.)

```
m_pPatches= new SGEOMM_PATCH [SQUARE( m_iNumPatchesPerSide )];
```

Next, although it is not a necessary part of initialization, I want to calculate the maximum level of detail that a patch can achieve. Notice that the maximum level of detail is the *least* detailed level, being that the *most* detailed level is 0. As the level increases, detail decreases.

$$p = \frac{h}{s}$$

Figure 5.11 *The equation for figuring out the number of patches for each side of the terrain mesh.*

Here are the calculations:

```
iDivisor= m_iPatchSize-1;
while( iDivisor>2 )
{
        iDivisor= iDivisor>>1;
        iLOD++;
}
```

All we are doing here is seeing how many loops it takes to get iDivisor down to 2. When iDivisor reaches 2, we cannot go down any further, and we have calculated the levels of detail we have at our disposal. For a 17 × 17 patch size, our maximum level of detail is 3, which means that we have four different levels of detail (0, 1, 2, and 3) to choose from for any single patch. That's it for initialization! Now we are going to move on to the tremendously large shutdown section.

Geomipmapping Shutdown

It's simple and routine to shut down the geomipmapping system. All we need to do is free the memory that we allocated for the patch buffer and reset all of the class's member variables.

Geomipmapping Maintenance

Unlike the terrain we've been working with for the past three chapters, CLOD terrain algorithms need to be updated every frame (which is why it's called *Continuous* Level of Detail). Most CLOD-based algorithms require a lot of maintenance work to be done during the update phase, but geomipmapping is not one of those. The work we have to do during our update function is quite minimal; it simply consists of figuring out which LOD our patch should be.

For the update function of our geomipmapping implementation, we need to update every patch; therefore, we need to make a pair of for loops:

```
for( z=0; z<m_iNumPatchesPerSide; z++ )
{
        for( x=0; x<m_iNumPatchesPerSide; x++ )
        {
```

The first thing that we need to do inside this loop is calculate the distance from the viewer's location (the camera eye position) to the center of the current patch. This calculation should look familiar from your high school math classes, where they drilled the distance formula into your head. Just in case you're like me and you slept through all of those classes, here it is again (see Figure 5.12):

$$dist = \sqrt{(x_2 - x_1)^2 + (y_2 - y_1)^2 + (z_2 - z_1)^2}$$

Figure 5.12 *The 3D distance formula.*

With that equation in mind, check out Figure 5.13 to see what variables we are going to plug into the equation.

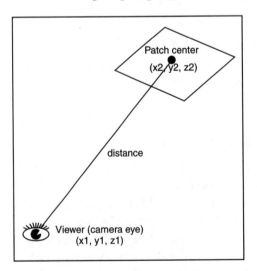

Figure 5.13 *The variables involved in the distance calculation (from the viewer to the current patch's center).*

Here is the same distance calculation in code:

```
m_pPatches[iPatch].m_fDistance= sqrtf(
                        SQUARE( ( fX-camera.m_vecEyePos[0] ) )+
                        SQUARE( ( fY-camera.m_vecEyePos[1] ) )+
                        SQUARE( ( fZ-camera.m_vecEyePos[2] ) ) );
```

After we have calculated the distance from the viewer, we can figure out what level of detail to give the patch. In the code, I figured out the level by hard-coding the distances. (I did this in the code segment a few paragraphs away; you might want to just skim ahead a bit to see what I'm talking about.) For your engine, though, you'll want a more rigorous way to figure out what level of detail a patch should be. For instance, in the geomipmapping whitepaper, Willem de Boer presents a screen-pixel determination algorithm so that when a patch changes its level of detail, too much *popping* won't be present.

Popping is when a polygonal object changes to a different level of detail. This change might or might not be evident. For instance, changing from a level 1 patch to a level 0 patch doesn't induce much popping because a level 1 patch is still decently detailed (for a 17×17 patch, at least). However, changing from a level 3 patch to a level 2 patch causes quite a bit of popping because you're going from 8 triangles to 32. Although that's the same ratio of triangles added as in the first patch, it is more evident in the level 3 to level 2 change. One of the major goals in any CLOD algorithm is to reduce or even eliminate popping completely. We will talk more about this a bit later.

Anyway, for my geomipmapping implementation for this book, I am simply hard-coding the LOD distance changes. (I want to leave the exercises open for you, the reader. Yes, I know I'm a nice guy.) Here is the LOD-changing code snippet:

```
if( m_pPatches[iPatch].m_fDistance<500 )
    m_pPatches[iPatch].m_iLOD= 0;

else if( m_pPatches[iPatch].m_fDistance<1000 )
    m_pPatches[iPatch].m_iLOD= 1;

else if( m_pPatches[iPatch].m_fDistance<2500 )
    m_pPatches[iPatch].m_iLOD= 2;
```

```
else if( m_pPatches[iPatch].m_fDistance>=2500 )
    m_pPatches[iPatch].m_iLOD= 3;
```

These distances make for an effective combination of speed and detail. If the demo is a bit sluggish on your video card, you might want to change these distances, but don't. We will make some speed optimizations later in this chapter, so don't despair! That's all there is to updating geomipmapping patches... for now, at least. Now it's time to get to the fun part of any terrain implementation: rendering it!

Geomipmapping Rendering

This is probably the hardest section you'll come across in this chapter, and it's not too bad. It's a bit complicated at times, but I'll step you through it.

Splitting Things Up a Bit

The easiest way to render everything that we need to render is by splitting up the individual rendering routines a bit so that the code doesn't become too bloated. This might increase function overhead a bit, but as long as we do things smartly, it won't be too bad.

The way I figure it, the geomipmapping class should have a high-level rendering function, in addition to several lower-level ones, in succession. For instance, the highest level rendering function is Render. Following Render is RenderPatch and then RenderFan. RenderVertex comes in at the lowest level. Using these functions, we increase function overhead a bit, but we decrease the ugliness of our code significantly. The trade-off is worth it. If you are having a hard time grasping the design I plan to use, check out Figure 5.14. As for implementing our rendering system, let's start low and work our way up.

The RenderVertex Function

The system's vertex-rendering function isn't anything special, but to be fair, it's a small function. We will call it often, which makes it a perfect inline function. RenderVertex sets the vertex's color, which is based on the shading value that is extracted from the lightmap and multiplied by the respective RGB value of the light's color. Then RenderVertex sends the texture coordinates to the rendering API (for detail mapping, if needed, and for the color texture). After that, you simply need to send the scaled vertex coordinate to the rendering API. That's it!

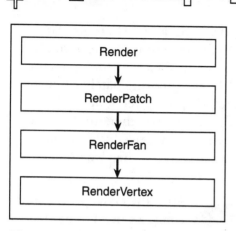

Figure 5.14 *The rendering architecture for the* Geomipmapping *class.*

The RenderFan Function

Each geomipmapping patch is broken down into several fans, whether they are 1 patch or 256 patches. Using this function clears up much of the code used in RenderPatch, which is discussed in the next section.

All the patch-rendering function is doing is rendering a single triangle fan. Therefore, the function needs to be able to accept the fan's center as an argument and the size of one side of the fan so that the function can render it. RendorFan also needs to obtain neighbor information from the patch. Well, sort of. The neighbor information is for the individual fan. If the patch needs to omit a vertex due to a coarser patch on its right side, but the current fan is in the middle of the patch, then the neighbor structure shows all neighbors as true. (Only fans on the right edge of the patch need to worry about vertex omission.) If the fan is being rendered, however, vertex omissions are needed. For instance, if the fan were on the right edge of the patch, and the patch to the right of the current patch was of a coarser LOD, then the current fan would need to omit the rendering of the right vertex.

The RenderPatch Function

The patch-rendering function is of critical importance to the whole rendering system because without rendering a patch, you don't see the terrain. Most of the crack-prevention steps take place in this function, with the rest (vertex omission) taking place in the RenderFan function.

Remember the pseudo-code I showed you back in "Where Art Thou Crack?" Well, this is where we need to implement it. We need to fill out a "neighbor structure," which is a simple data structure that contains four boolean flags for whether the neighboring patches (left, right, upper, and lower patches) are of a higher level of detail than the current one. If the neighbor is marked as true, then we can render as normal on that side of patch because we don't need to take special measures to prevent cracks. If it's marked as false, then we do need to take special measures.

> **NOTE**
>
> When we talk about a "higher level of detail" in this chapter, we mean a "lower detail level." This is because our level system starts high (a low amount of detail) and gets more detailed as the level gets lower, ending with level 0 as the most detailed. Just don't get confused when we talk about high/low levels of detail.

After the crack-prevention steps, we need to figure out how to start rendering the triangle-fans. This is a slight bit more complicated than it might sound, but it's not too difficult. The hardest part about this is trying to figure out the distance between the centers of the triangle fans. After that's done, we're good as gold!

How do we figure out the distance between each fan center? Well, the way I went about it, although it looks slightly odd, is by starting with the individual patch size and trying to figure out what to divide that by to get the length between each fan's center. I started out the divisor the size of a patch and then did a while loop to figure out how much to divide the total patch size by. For instance, if the patch were level 0, we would divide the individual patch size by itself, which produces a length of 1 unit between each fan that we render. (We do not want to scale vertices until we get down to the RenderVertex function.) For a patch of level 1, the distance between each fan would be 2 units, for level 2 would be 8 units, and so on. The code for the previous calculations looks like this:

```
fDivisor= ( float )m_iPatchSize;
fSize   = ( float )m_iPatchSize;
iLOD    = m_pPatches[iPatch].m_iLOD;
```

```
//find out how many fan divisions we are going to have
while( iLOD-->=0 )
    iDivisor= fDivisor/2.0f;

//the size between the center of each triangle fan
fSize/= fDivisor;
```

The calculations here aren't entirely correct, though; when we use
them, they produce terrain that looks like Figure 5.15.

Figure 5.15 *Oops! It looks like some wrong calculations were performed!*

What went wrong with those calculations? Well, we did one simple
thing wrong. We want the divisor variable, fDivisor, to be a power of
two. Remember that when the divisor was equal to the patch size, the
distance between fans for a level 0 patch was 1 unit? Well, going from
center to center, we need at least a 2-unit interval (see Figure 5.16).

You see how the pair of fans on top in Figure 5.16 overlaps each other
(producing a rather ugly result) with a one-unit interval and how the
two fans on bottom fit together perfectly with the two-unit interval?
Well, we need to change the previous fan center interval calculations
so that the minimum interval between patches is 2 units. How do we
do this, you ask? It's rather simple. We just set the initial divisor variable to the patch size minus 1, which always makes the divisor variable
a power of two, thereby fixing all the problems we were previously
having. Check out the new code. (fDivisor turned into iDivisor so that
we could speed up the calculations a bit.)

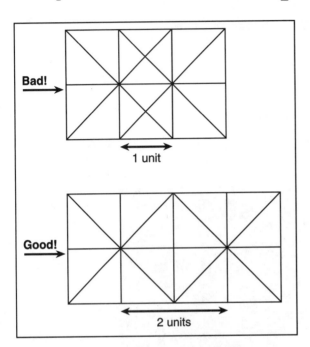

Figure 5.16 *A one-unit interval between fan centers versus a two-unit interval between patch centers.*

```
fSize   = ( float )m_iPatchSize;
iDivisor= m_iPatchSize-1;
iLOD    = m_pPatches[iPatch].m_iLOD;

//find out how many fan divisions we are going to have
while( iLOD-->=0 )
    iDivisor= iDivisor>>1;

//the size between the center of each triangle fan
fSize/= iDivisor;
```

After that is done, rendering the patch's triangle fans becomes trivial. You just need to be sure that you start rendering at half of fSize because that is where the first fan's center will be. We need to check whether each fan needs to omit vertices. That means we need to use the patch neighbor structure's information that we filled out earlier and apply it to the fans being rendered on the edge of each patch, as is shown next:

```
//if this fan is in the left row, we might need to
//adjust its rendering to prevent cracks
if( x==fHalfSize )
    fanNeighbor.m_bLeft= patchNeighbor.m_bLeft;
else
    fanNeighbor.m_bLeft= true;


//if this fan is in the bottom row, we might need to
//adjust its rendering to prevent cracks
if( z==fHalfSize )
    fanNeighbor.m_bDown= patchNeighbor.m_bDown;
else
    fanNeighbor.m_bDown= true;


//if this fan is in the right row, we might need to
//adjust its rendering to prevent cracks
if( x>=( m_iPatchSize-fHalfSize ) )
    fanNeighbor.m_bRight= patchNeighbor.m_bRight;
else
    fanNeighbor.m_bRight= true;


//if this fan is in the top row, we might need to
//adjust its rendering to prevent cracks
if( z>=( m_iPatchSize-fHalfSize ) )
    fanNeighbor.m_bUp= patchNeighbor.m_bUp;
else
    fanNeighbor.m_bUp= true;


//render the triangle fan
RenderFan( ( PX*m_iPatchSize )+x, ( PZ*m_iPatchSize )+z,
           fSize, fanNeighbor, bMultiTe x, bDetail );
```

By filling out a separate fan neighbor structure, we don't have to keep redoing the patch's neighbor structure. The fan neighbor structure is then sent to the fan-rendering function, where it is used to find out whether any vertices need to be omitted from rendering. That is it for all of the low-level rendering functions. Now we need to briefly discuss the class's high-level Render function, which is the one that users will be using. We can unleash demo5_1 upon the world!

The Render Function

Well, we're just about finished with our simple geomipmapping implementation. Are you getting excited? I know I am!

In the high-level rendering function, we need to loop through all of the patches and call the RenderPatch function, but we're going to have three different patch-rendering loops. Remember our brute force implementation? We only need to make one rendering loop if the user has multitexturing enabled; however, if the user does not have multitexturing enabled, we might need to make a texture map pass and a detail map pass. Two different rendering passes for a terrain implementation is *never* a good thing, though, so one option is to avoid the detail mapping pass if the user does not have multitexturing support. You should already be familiar with this concept if you've been reading this book's chapters in succession from the beginning. The only thing you have to do is loop through all the patches and use the RenderPatch function to render them.

That's it! We are finished making the basic geomipmapping implementation. Check out demo5_1 (on the CD under Code\Chapter 5\demo5_1) and look at a sample screenshot from that demo in Figure 5.17. It shows the textured/detail-mapped image on the left and the wireframe of that same image on the right. Notice in the wireframe half how the patches are more detailed near you and less detailed farther away. *That* is the beauty of a CLOD algorithm!

Problems Exist to Be Fixed

Yeah, yeah, I know. There are some problems with the geomipmapping implementation we just finished making. For instance, unless you're on a really high-end card, you probably experienced a horribly bad frame rate on the previous demo. (I'm on a GeForce 4 TI4600, the best card on the market at the time of writing, and I got a steady 45–50 frames per second with the demo.) The demo also suffered from some popping when patches of terrain changed their level of detail. We will fix all this and more in the upcoming sections, so don't worry!

Adding a Bit of Juice to the Engine

First, I think we should speed up our implementation. Speeding things up is easy. It simply involves doing some frustum culling. And

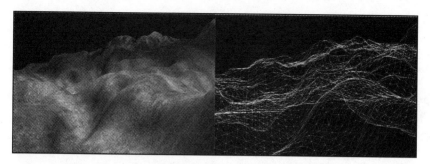

Figure 5.17 *A texture and detail mapped terrain screenshot (left) and its corresponding wireframe image (right), taken from demo5_1.*

because our terrain is split up into several patches, our best bet is to just cull those patches against the view-frustum, which means that not many tests will have to be done.

Cull Like You've Never Culled Before... Again

We're going to be doing some basic frustum culling here. I added some frustum calculation functionality to the CCAMERA class based on some information in Mark Morley's article "Frustum Culling in OpenGL," which I consider *the* best frustum culling tutorial I've seen on the Internet. (You can find it at http://www.markmorley.com/opengl/frustumculling.html.) Yes, I'll admit it, my math knowledge isn't too great (notice the lack of complicated math throughout this book!), but that's probably a good thing—unless you're a huge math junkie, in which case, I should probably expect some hate mail.

Anyway, here are the basics of what we are going to be doing. We are going to be culling a patch of terrain against the view frustum (Figure 5.18 in case you need a visual refresher) so that we eliminate any extra CPU/GPU work that ends up going to waste. (If the viewer can't see it, there's no point in rendering/updating it.)

We need to test a patch of terrain against that frustum. To do this, we make an Axis-Aligned Bounding Box (AABB) out of the patch. (Actually, we make more along the lines of a cube.) Then we want to test it against the view frustum. To calculate the patch's dimensions, we take the center and one scaled size variable (see Figure 5.19).

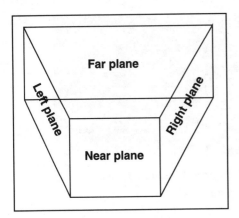

Figure 5.18 *The view frustum.*

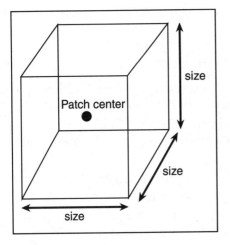

Figure 5.19 *Making a cube out of a geomipmapping patch to test against the view frustum.*

Because we're dealing with only the patch center here, you need to take half of the size passed as a function argument (to the Cube-Frustum intersection) and figure out the corners of the cube based on that. We could also get a more precise box, but in my experiments with culling, the extra "space buffer" is necessary so that a viewer doesn't see inconsistencies in the terrain (such as a patch that *is* slightly visible but ends up getting culled anyway).

Now that you know more about culling and its practical uses for terrain, check out demo5_2 (on the CD under Code\Chapter 5\demo5_2) and witness for yourself how much faster things have gotten. For instance, in Figure 5.20, out of about 910 patches, we see only 369. For the demo, I was getting a steady frame rate (80–120fps), and this was with a heightmap that was twice as large as the one in demo5_1. Not too shabby!

Figure 5.20 *A screenshot from demo5_2.*

Pop Today, Gone Tomorrow

The next problem we get to tackle is more complicated than the previous one. Our goal is to reduce or—even better—eliminate popping. There are several ways to go about this, and I will present the theory behind two of them. The actual implementation of these solutions is up to you, though.

Morph It! And Morph It Good!

The first solution to the popping problem is called geomorphing. Although that name sounds like something you'd expect to hear in an anime about giant mechs, it has absolutely nothing to do with giant

multistory robots that are capable of mass destruction. *Geomorphing* is
actually the process of gradually morphing vertices in a set of polygons
(like our geomipmapping patch) that are changing their level of
detail. I personally think the mech thing sounded like more fun,
but the actual meaning of geomorphing is far more useful.

Why is this useful, you ask? It is quite simple, actually. You see, when a
patch is of a low level of detail, it approximates the heights of several
areas (see Figure 5.21). And, in the figure, areas where the patch is
approximating values are marked with a black dot.

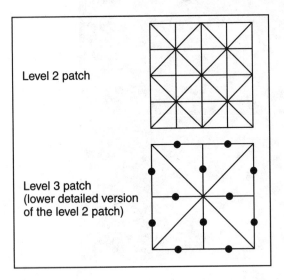

Level 2 patch

Level 3 patch
(lower detailed version
of the level 2 patch)

Figure 5.21 *How a lower-level patch approximates
height values for several vertices of the lower level patch.*

You see how many black dots are on the lower patch in the image?
Well, that's how many height values are being approximated by the
lower-detailed patch. The approximate values are close to the real value,
but not close enough. Therefore, when the level 3 patch subdivides into
the level 2 patch (or vice-versa), popping occurs; that's because those
approximated values are being "replaced" by the true values (or the
true values are being replaced by the approximated values).

Geomorphing fixes this problem by figuring out how far off the
approximated value is from the true value and interpolating it from
the approximated value to the true value over a series of about 255
steps. (Or vice versa... again. Okay, from here on out, I'm going to

assume that we're subdividing the patch. If you're merging a patch, just reverse all of the calculations.) To calculate the number of units you need to move every step, just use this equation:

$$geo = \frac{(to\text{-}from)}{numSteps}$$

Figure 5.22 *Equation to calculate the geomorphing value.*

In the equation, "to" is the real value that you are going to, "from" is the approximate value that you are going from, and "numSteps" is the number of steps you want for the geomorphing to take place, which I suggested to be 255. This whole process is explained visually in Figure 5.23.

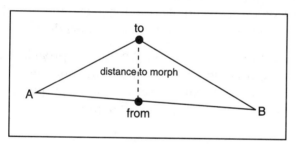

Figure 5.23 *Geomorphing explained.*

Well, that's it. Geomorphing is a simple concept, and you can implement it in several different ways. (I didn't want to limit your imagination, which is why I didn't implement it myself). Go have some fun with it, but make sure that you come back and read the next section, which helps reduce popping in your terrain implementation even more.

Should Lights Make a Popping Noise?

The answer is no, although that is not important right now. What *is* important is that we reduce popping in our terrain implementation a bit. Now, although it's true that a majority of the popping that occurs when changing LOD levels can be fixed by geomorphing, another problem is that we're using gouraud (per-vertex) lighting! Although this might not sound like a big deal, it is. With every LOD switch, the lighting applied to a patch gets more/less detailed, which should not happen. Fortunately, fixing this problem is trivial, and you can handle it a few different ways.

One way of fixing the problem is to integrate the terrain's lightmap with the terrain's texture map. This allows you to do lighting and texturing in one rendering pass. Unfortunately, this means that you have to make your lightmap and texture map the same resolution for optimal results. Therefore, if you want to dynamically change lighting, you have to dynamically change the texture map too, which is rather expensive.

Another way of fixing this problem is by making a separate lightmap texture pass. This treats the lightmap as a texture, eliminates the per-vertex lighting, and allows you to dynamically update it without bothering with the texture map. Unfortunately, this means that your users need at least 3 multitexturing units for this approach to be efficient. Furthermore, even if your user has 2 texture units, doing 2 rendering passes is not really a good idea. Multipass rendering is no big deal for small models, but for *huge* polygonal sets of data, like a terrain mesh, it is a big deal.

The solution you go with is completely up to you. The first approach is great if you don't need to do dynamic slope-lighting or lightmapping, and the second approach is great if you know your user has a graphics card that supports 3 or more texture units. Use extra texture units with caution.

Summary

Well, it's been a long chapter, but you made it. Congratulations! In this chapter, you learned all about general CLOD terrain, but you also learned about the geomipmapping CLOD terrain algorithm. You learned how to speed up geomipmapping and how to reduce popping caused by a change in LOD. Keep all these techniques in mind as you read the next couple of chapters. Brace yourself: Up next is a CLOD algorithm based on a quadtree structure.

References

1 de Boer, Willem H. "Fast Terrain Rendering Using Geometrical Mipmapping." October 2000. http://www.flipcode.com/tutorials/geomipmaps.pdf.

CHAPTER 6

CLIMBING THE QUADTREE

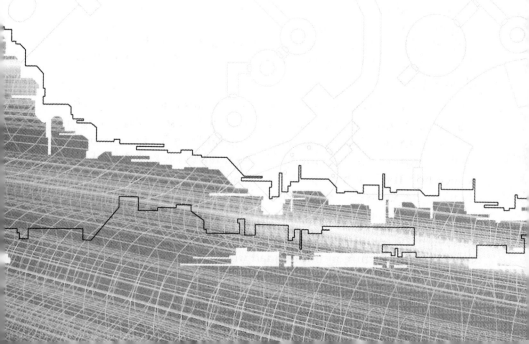

We are one-third of the way through our CLOD algorithm coverage in this book. In this chapter, you will learn about Stefan Roettger's quadtree terrain algorithm. This algorithm is very cool and very fast. Now that you've read Chapter 5, "Geomipmapping for the CLOD Impaired," the quadtree terrain algorithm shouldn't be too hard to pick up. When you understand one CLOD algorithm, the difficulty of learning new CLOD algorithms is greatly reduced.

The agenda for this chapter looks like this:

- Explanation of what a quadtree is
- Application of a typical quadtree structure to terrain
- Implementation of the quadtree algorithm

So, without further ado... Wait a second—I already used that one. Hmmm... Let's just start the chapter.

Quads Do Grow on Trees

Whoever told you money doesn't grow on trees was sadly mistaken. In contrast, quads do have a tendency to grow on trees. Those trees are aptly named quadtrees, and that is what we're going to be talking about in the next section, and the section after that, and, well, this whole chapter.

A quadtree is a 2D data structure, which makes it ideal for terrain. Yes, I did say 2D and not 3D, which might make you start scratching your head about why a 2D data structure is good for a 3D terrain engine. Well, what you need to remember is that terrain is largely a 2D object. Notice how the heightmaps that we load are not 3D data sets; rather, they are 2D data sets, and our terrain runs off of those 2D data sets. A quadtree is perfect for managing the polygons of a terrain engine.

You might be asking yourself, "What is a quadtree exactly?" Well, it's simple, really. Picture a simple quad with a single point in it, as shown in Figure 6.1.

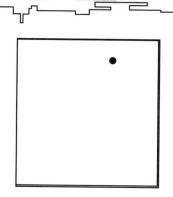

Figure 6.1 *A simple quad with a point in it.*

Now imagine that the quad is full of objects. All you want to do is focus on that one little point; you could care less about anything else. If that were the case, you wouldn't want to group the point together with all of the other objects. You'd want to get it into the smallest group that you possibly could. So, you subdivide that little quad one level, as shown in Figure 6.2.

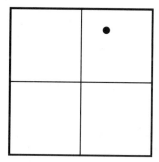

Figure 6.2 *A subdivided quad with a point in it.*

That's a little better, but now that we have 3/4 of the parent quad eliminated, we need to focus a bit more in depth on the remaining node. We want to subdivide *only* the upper-right node this time around, as shown in Figure 6.3.

Now we're getting somewhere! We could use one more subdivision, though. Remember: The more detail the better, despite what any one else ever told you. The final step in our little quad subdivision battle is shown in Figure 6.4.

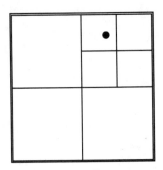

Figure 6.3 *Now the quad is getting somewhere, with a decent level of detail around the area that we want.*

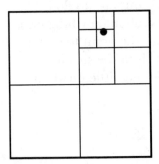

Figure 6.4 *The final level of subdivision in our quest to… subdivide.*

That was nice and all, but what was the point? Well, the point is this: You just subdivided a quad tree down to the necessary level of detail that you need for that point. What we were just doing is what we will be doing throughout this chapter. We'll start with a simple quad, as in Figure 6.1, and end with a fully triangulated terrain landscape. As we talk about the quadtree structure as it relates to our terrain, don't forget the simple explanation that I just gave you. It's all the same concept—just different applications!

Think Outside of the Quad!

Our quadtree explanation and implementation are based off of an excellent paper written by Stefan Roettger, "Real-Time Generation of Continuous Levels of Detail for Height Fields.[1]" The conference paper (which was published in the WSCG98 proceedings) is a detailed analysis of Roettger's algorithm, and it's definitely a must-read. In fact, I suggest you read it now either by checking the paper on the Web (the link is at the end of this chapter) or by simply looking at the copy I placed on this book's accompanying CD (Algorithm Whitepapers\quadtree.pdf).

Simply the Basics... Again

There is so much to discuss that it's hard to know where to start. Well, the beginning is always nice. I'm going to split this chapter into three sections, the first of which, "Quads Don't Grow on Trees," has already been covered. The next section is the one you are currently reading, which is going to cover the theory behind the quadtree algorithm in three different phases. Then the final section of the chapter will cover implementation. With that said, let's continue on with the basic theory section.

Life in the Matrix... The Quadtree Matrix

The quadtree algorithm is completely run off of an underlying quadtree matrix. This matrix matches the size of the heightmap that it is running off of and contains a boolean value for every possible node in the quadtree. For instance, similar to the whitepaper, let's base the matrix off of a 9×9 heightmap, as shown in Figure 6.5.

```
? ? ? ? ? ? ? ? ?
? 1 ? 1 ? 0 ? 1 ?
? ? 1 ? ? ? 1 ? ?
? 0 ? 0 ? 0 ? 0 ?
? ? ? ? 1 ? ? ? ?
? ? ? ? ? ? ? ? ?
? ? 0 ? ? ? 0 ? ?
? ? ? ? ? ? ? ? ?
? ? ? ? ? ? ? ? ?
```

Figure 6.5 *A sample boolean "quad matrix" for use in the quadtree algorithm.*

It's a bunch of little 0s, 1s, and question marks, but what does it all mean? Well, simply put, all these characters stand for node centers. Each 0 and 1 represents whether a center is enabled (1) or disabled (0). The question marks represent centers that aren't in consideration, which means that we haven't subdivided far enough down into the quadtree to "care" about those centers. I bet you're asking yourself, "What does that look like after it's tessellated?" Well, let me show you in Figure 6.6. And in case you weren't asking yourself that question, I'm just going to continue on pretending that you did.

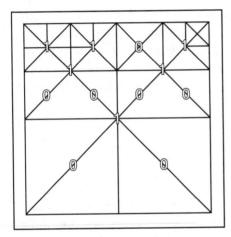

Figure 6.6 *Sample tessellation from the quadtree matrix presented in Figure 6.5.*

As you can see from the figure, the tessellation corresponds exactly to the quadtree matrix. However, what the matrix doesn't show is how the polygons in the tessellated mesh need to adjust themselves to prevent cracking. We'll get to that later. Anyway, with the previous explanation in mind, let's continue on.

Viewing the Matrix in an Environmentally Safe Fashion

We will be rendering the quad matrix in a fashion that you might or might not be familiar with. We need to start off by rendering the root quad node. Then we are going to recursively render its children's nodes, and then those children nodes will render their children nodes. After we reach a leaf node (a quad node with no children), we will render it as a full or partial triangle fan. Rendering is a redundant function in that it will call itself numerous times. (It's just a bit selfish like that.) In Figure 6.7, we'll examine the rendering process by picking apart Figure 6.6 and seeing how to render that mesh.

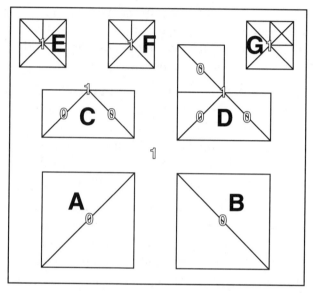

Figure 6.7 *Picking apart the mesh from Figure 6.6 for our rendering purposes.*

For rendering, we'd have to make seven calls to our node-rendering function (we want to render one node at a time), once for each lettered node. To prevent cracking, we're going to have to deal with the famous vertex omission technique that we talked about in Chapter 5. In fact, nothing really changes from Chapter 5 because we're still dealing with triangle fans, so when we need to prevent cracking, we just omit rendering a single vertex and continue on with the fan.

Similar to the previous algorithm, we will always be checking to see whether an adjacent node is of a lower level of detail than the current node. If it is, we have some vertex omission to do. None of this should seem too foreign to you, but it's important to remember that this technique only works if the adjacent node's level of detail does not differ by more than one level.

Gotta Keep 'Em Generated!

For those who know the song "Gotta Keep 'Em Separated" by the Offspring, this section title works well. For those who don't, well... you're missing out. Before a scene can be rendered, we need to generate the mesh. This algorithm, unlike the geomipmapping one discussed in Chapter 5, requires more involved updating. In every frame, we need to start high up on the quadtree (at the parent node) and work our way down the tree, seeing if we need more detail, less detail, and so on. This is called a *top-down* approach. Makes sense, doesn't it?

What we're going to do in our "refinement" step (we can't really call it "updating" because we start from scratch every frame) is test each node to see if it can or cannot be subdivided. Then we store the result in the quadtree matrix. If the node *can* be subdivided, and we have not yet reached the maximum level of detail, then we want to recurse further down the tree and do the same tests on all the node's children.

We need to expand on this whole "subdivision test" thing a bit. We need to discuss some requirements. First, like any good CLOD algorithm, we want to make sure that our mesh's detail decreases as the camera eye gets further away from it. This is ensured by using the equation shown in Figure 6.8, which is found in Roettger's whitepaper:

$$\frac{1}{d} < C$$

Figure 6.8 *The Global Resolution Criteria equation, which ensures that the quadtree mesh is the right level of detail.*

In the equation, l is the distance from the center of the current node to the camera eye, d is the length of the current node's edge, and C is a constant to control the overall level of detail for the mesh. We're going to be measuring the distance from the node's center to the camera a bit differently from the way we did it in Chapter 5. This time, we're going to use something called the L^1-Norm to calculate the distance. It's a faster version of the distance formula we used in Chapter 5, but it's linear rather than quadratic like the L^2-Norm we used before. See Figure 6.9.

$$d = |x_2 - x_1| + |y_2 - y_1| + |z_2 - z_1|$$

Figure 6.9 *The L¹-Norm distance calculation equation.*

You see, it isn't that much different from the distance equation from Chapter 5. The only real difference is that we're not bothering to square the individual component calculations, and we're saving ourselves the trouble of a square root. Other than that, not much has changed.

Anyway, all that the previous equation does is balance the total amount of visible detail across the entire terrain mesh. The constant C allows us control of the minimum resolution of the mesh. Roettger advised, in the conference paper that we are basing our implementation off of, that this value be set to nine as a default. However, it's important to note that as C increases, the total number of vertices per frame grows quadratically.

After doing all of this, we need to calculate what the whitepaper calls f, which is the final step in determining whether to subdivide a node. The way we are going to be calculating f for the basic implementation (demo6_1 later on) is a little different from the calculations for f for the second "go" at an implementation (demo6_2.). So, for the basic theory that we're talking about right now, I'm going to focus on the simplified calculations, shown in Figure 6.10.

$$f = \frac{1}{d \bullet C \bullet MAX(c, 1)}$$

Figure 6.10 *Early equation for calculating f.*

You should already know what l, d, and C are, but you don't know what c is. Okay, I'll tell you. c is related to C, but whereas C is the minimum global resolution constant, c is the desired resolution constant.

The real question, however, is what f has to do with anything. Well, f is the final step in deciding whether we want to subdivide a node. After you calculate the value for it, you have one simple thing to test for:

```
If f<1
    Subdivide node
```

You then would store true in the quadtree matrix for the current node and continue to refine the node's children. That's it for the basic quadtree theory. Let's move on to the next section.

Propagation Propaganda

This theory section is about how to improve the tessellation of your quadtree implementation. In the previous section, we talked about general tessellation. Although general tessellation works decently, a quadtree implementation is capable of so much more than just "normal" tessellation. We're going to discuss how we can add more detail to our mesh in areas that require it. For instance, we might want a spiky patch of terrain to have a lot more detail than just a regular flat patch of land. Doing this requires a bit of extra work on our parts though, so if you don't think that the extra detail is needed, feel free to skip ahead to the next section.

We are going to be preprocessing a value called d2 for every node. We'll then store a propagation value in the quad matrix, which we'll want to change to make each entry into a byte rather than simply a boolean flag, for later use (during tessellation). We are going to be calculating five d2 values for every node, and we'll find the maximum value of those five. Look at Figure 6.11 to see where the d2 values need to be calculated. (An X is placed in those places.)

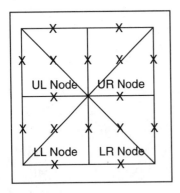

Figure 6.11 *An X marks the d2 calculation spot!*

For any d2 calculation, all you need to do is calculate the average between the two vertices that the X lies between (because that is the current approximated height that the viewer sees). Then you need to find the absolute difference between that value and the true height at that point. That's your d2 value.

Next, we need to take anticracking precautions. In this step, we want to make sure that surrounding nodes do not differ by more than one level of detail. To do this, we're going to do things a bit differently from the rest of the algorithm. Instead of taking a top-down approach, we're going to take a bottom-up approach and start at the lowest level of detail and work our way up. We'll be calculating the surface roughness and d2 values for the lowest nodes, storing the information, and propagating up the quadtree.

NOTE

The d2 propagation values should be scaled to a range of [0, 1] and then set to a more byte-friendly range of [0, 255].

By preprocessing the quadtree in a bottom-up fashion, the level of detail difference between nodes is kept to a range of less than or equal to 1. This makes sure that cracks can be avoided just by skipping necessary vertices. If there is a difference in the level of detail that is greater than 1, the d2 values of the coarser node can be simply adjusted to conform to the lower detailed node.

Cull Like You've Never Culled Before... Again

I promise that the section headings for the next chapter will be more original. Anyway, this section will be rather short. You know the basics of frustum culling, and the only change between the culling in the previous algorithm and the culling in this algorithm is how we're going to handle things. You see, in the previous algorithm, we had to cull *every* patch every frame. When we cull one quadtree node, we potentially eliminate a whole set of other nodes. For instance, check out Figure 6.12.

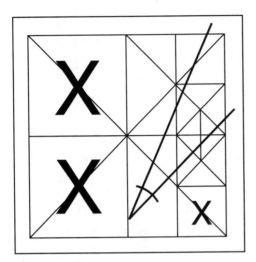

Figure 6.12 *Frustum culling of a sample quadtree terrain patch.*

As you can see, the two large nodes to the left of the camera eye are completely culled without even bothering to test their children. On a large heightmap, this saves a lot of processing time. It allows the GPU to take more information, which is ultimately what we want. Other than the previous culling concept, however, everything is the same as it was in the Chapter 5. This wraps up the theory section of the chapter. It's time to move on to implementation.

Hug the Quadtree, Love the Quadtree, *Be* the Quadtree

After spending the past few pages on the theory behind Roettger's quadtree algorithm, we are finally going to implement it. This section is *only* about implementation, so theory will not be discussed. If you forget why a certain piece of code works the way it does, refer back to the theory section for the explanation.

Implementing the Basics

To start off with this implementation, it's good to create the CQUADTREE class. Let's not waste time!

Get Some Class!

For the most part, the class is rather simple, consisting of "helper" inline functions to keep the code clean, three member variables, and five main functions. The class's member variables consist of a boolean buffer to hold the quadtree matrix, a variable to represent the minimum global resolution, and desired global resolution variables.

As far as member functions go, we need the now-trademark `Init`, `Shutdown`, `Update`, and `Render` functions, but we also need two node-manipulation functions: `RefineNode` and `RenderNode`. Let's get coding!

Quadtree Initialization and Shutdown

The initialization function is standard fare, nothing special. All we really need to do is allocate memory for the quadtree buffer and set all of its contents to `true`. That's all there really is to the initialization function. I told you it was nothing special. However, it is *very* important that you remember to initialize the entire matrix to `true`; if you don't, you will get some nasty-looking results.

Shutdown of the quadtree system is also ridiculously simple. Just free the memory that you allocated for the quadtree matrix and you're set.

Quadtree Updating and Rendering

These high-level class functions are really simple. For the class's `Update` function, you're just making a single call to `RefineNode`. Because the function is recursive, you just have to start the thing off by refining the parent node. Pass the parent's center and its size, and you're set!

The rendering function is similar to Chapter 5's high-level rendering function. The difference is that instead of looping through each patch and rendering it, you just need to make one call to `RenderNode`. Similar to its refined brother, this is also a recursive function, so by rendering the parent node, you start off the recursion down the quadtree. All the rendering function needs to do is send the right texture/detail map information so that the low-level `RenderVertex` function (the same function from Chapter 5) knows what to do.

Refining a Quad Node

Now we're talking! Here you will learn how to refine a single quad node (although the function is recursive, so you're actually refining several quad nodes). You already know most of what you need to about how to refine a quad node if you read the theory section earlier in this chapter. You did read that section, didn't you?

We're going to start the refining process by figuring out the distance between the node center and the camera eye position, using the L^1-Norm that we discussed earlier.

```
distance= ( float )( fabs( cameraEye[0]-x )+
            ( fabs(cameraEye [1]-GetQuadMatrixData( iX+1, iZ ) )+
            ( fabs(cameraEye [2]-z ) );
```

With that calculated, we can go on to calculate f as was shown earlier in this chapter. When that is calculated, we can figure out if we can subdivide the current node:

```
f= fViewDistance/( ( float )iEdgeLength*m_fMinResolution*
    MAX( m_fDesiredResolution*GetQuadMatrixData( iX-1, iZ )/3,
                                        1.0f ) );
```

We can find out about subdividing the current node by checking to see if f is less than 1. If it is, then the current node can be subdivided; if it's not, it's a leaf node.

```
if( f<1.0f )
    bSubdivide= true;
else
    bSubdivide= false;
```

```
//store whether or not the current node gets subdivided
m_bpQuadMtrx[GetMatrixIndex( iX, iZ )]= bSubdivide;
```

If the node is subdivided, it isn't a leaf node (obviously), which means it has children that need to be further refined. The exception to this rule is if the current node has an edge length of three units. If it has an edge length of three units, it is the lowest possible node on the quadtree, and we cannot recurse any further down the tree.

```
if( bSubdivide )
{
```

```
//else, we need to recurse down further into the quadtree
if( !iEdgeLength<=3 )
{
    fChildOffset    = ( float )( ( iEdgeLength-1 ) >> 2 );
    iChildEdgeLength= ( iEdgeLength+1 ) >> 1;

    //refine the various child nodes
    //lower left
    RefineNode( x-fChildOffset, z-fChildOffset,
                iChildEdgeLength, camera );

    //lower right
    RefineNode( x+fChildOffset, z-fChildOffset,
                iChildEdgeLength, camera );

    //upper left
    RefineNode( x-fChildOffset, z+fChildOffset,
                iChildEdgeLength, camera );

    //upper right
    RefineNode( x+fChildOffset, z+fChildOffset,
                iChildEdgeLength, camera );
}
}
```

That's it for the node refine function. Basically, you're just checking
for a subdivision and storing the result. If you need to subdivide, you
recurse further down the quadtree. Next on our list is the rendering
function.

Rendering a Quad Node

Rendering is a rather long and drawn-out process (not to mention
repetitive), but don't let the daunting size of the rendering function
in demo6_1 (or the other demos for this chapter) fool you; rendering
is a lot simpler than it looks.

To start off the function, we're going to check whether the current
node we are rendering is of the highest level of detail (edge length of
3 units or less). If it is, we can just render it without special precautions.

Just remember to check to see whether the surrounding nodes are of a lower LOD; if they are, skip the vertex on that side of the fan.

If the current node is not of the highest level of detail, we have a bit more work to do. We're going to calculate the rendering code to figure out what kind of triangle fans to draw for the current node. To calculate this rendering code, we will be using the propagation values that are stored in our quadtree matrix, as shown next:

```
//calculate the bit-iFanCode for the fan
//arrangement (which fans need to be rendered)
//upper right
iFanCode = ( GetQuadMatrixData( iX+iChildOffset,
                                iZ+iChildOffset )!=0 )*8;


//upper left
iFanCode|= ( GetQuadMatrixData( iX-iChildOffset,
                                iZ+iChildOffset )!=0 )*4;


//lower left
iFanCode|= ( GetQuadMatrixData( iX-iChildOffset,
                                iZ-iChildOffset )!=0 )*2;


//lower right
iFanCode|= ( GetQuadMatrixData( iX+iChildOffset,
                                iZ-iChildOffset )!=0 );
```

After we calculate the rendering code, we can decide which fans need to be drawn. We're going to start off by checking whether we need to render a fan at all. This case would happen if all of the current node's children were to be rendered. Another trivial case is if only the lower-left/upper-right fans or the lower-right/upper-left fans need to be drawn. And the last trivial case is if we don't need to render any of the node's children at all, and we can just render the current node as one complete triangle fan.

There are other cases besides the trivial ones that we just mentioned. These consist of partial fans that need to be rendered across the quadtree. For instance, in Figure 6.13, a partial fan would need to render the bottom node, which consists of two disabled child nodes.

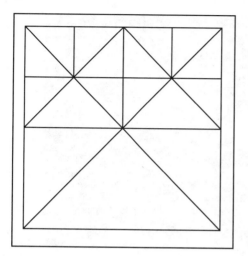

Figure 6.13 *A quadtree node that requires special rendering attention.*

The code for partial fan rendering is fairly routine, but it's also highly redundant and long. If you'd like to see it, check out the `RenderNode` function in quadtree.cpp in demo6_1. It's all there and heavily commented, so it will be self-explanatory.

After the partial fans are drawn, we need to figure out which children of the current node we need to recurse down to. When that is done, we're good as gold! And that wraps it up for the basic quadtree implementation. Go check out demo6_1 and Figures 6.14 and 6.15. Also check out Table 6.1 for a look at the demo's controls.

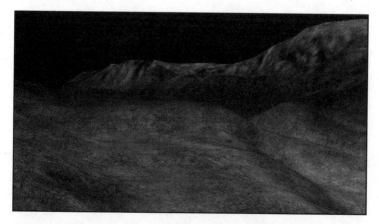

Figure 6.14 *Textured and detail mapped screenshot from demo6_1.*

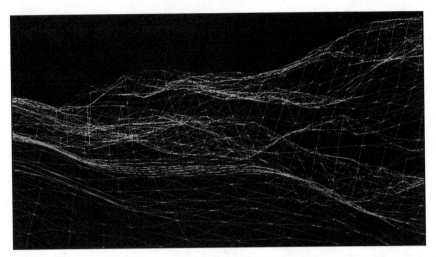

Figure 6.15 *Wireframe image of the terrain from Figure 6.14.*

Table 6.1 Controls for demo6_1

Key	Function
Escape / q	Quit the program
Up arrow	Move forward
Down arrow	Move backward
Right arrow	Strafe right
Left arrow	Strafe left
T	Toggle texture mapping
D	Toggle detail mapping
W	Render in wireframe mode
S	Render in solid/fill mode
+ / -	Increase/decrease mouse sensitivity
] / [	Increase/decrease movement sensitivity
1 / 2	Increase/decrease desired resolution
3 / 4	Increase/decrease minimum resolution

Complicating Things a Bit

Now it's time to implement the roughness propagation that we were talking about earlier. To do this, we need to increase the quadtree matrix's precision from a matrix of boolean values to a series of byte (unsigned char) values. Other than that, however, we don't need to change that much of the code from the Chapter 5. We're going to add one function that you'll want to add to your initialization procedure: PropagateRoughness.

Remember that for propagation, we want to take a bottom-up approach, which means that we want to start at the highest level of detail for the tree—nodes with an edge length of three units. Then we want to loop through all of the nodes and propagate their surface roughness.

```
//set the iEdgeLength to 3 (lowest length possible)
iEdgeLength= 3;

//start off at the lowest level of detail and traverse
//up to the highest node (lowest detail)
while( iEdgeLength<=m_iSize )
{
    //offset of node edges (since all edges are the same length
    iEdgeOffset= ( iEdgeLength-1 )>>1;

    //offset of the node's children's edges
    iChildOffset= ( iEdgeLength-1 )>>2;

    for( z=iEdgeOffset; z<m_iSize; z+=( iEdgeLength-1 ) )
    {
        for( x=iEdgeOffset; x<m_iSize; x+=( iEdgeLength-1 ) )
        {
```

With that being the basis for our loop, we can calculate the d2 value for the current node. As I said earlier, all you need to do is get the current approximation from two corner vertices and then subtract that by the true height at the point. Here is sample code from the calculation for the upper-mid vertex of a node:

```
d2= ( int )ceil( abs( ( (
    GetTrueHeightAtPoint( x-iEdgeOffset, z+iEdgeOffset )+
    GetTrueHeightAtPoint( x+iEdgeOffset, z+iEdgeOffset ) )>>1 )-
    GetTrueHeightAtPoint( x,              z+iEdgeOffset ) ) );
```

After you calculate the different d2 values, you need to get the maximum and make sure it is within the allowable boundary of 0–255. (That is the maximum precision that an `unsigned char` can get. I don't know about you, but I don't feel like spending more memory on making a quadtree matrix of higher-precision values.)

We want to figure out the general surface roughness of the current node instead of figuring out the approximate/real height. This is easy. All you're going to do is extract the height values from the current node's nine vertices. After you do that, you'll want to store the d2 value that you calculated in the current node's quadtree matrix entry. Then you can use the maximum height and the d2 value to propagate further up the quadtree.

The new quadtree value is applied in the `RefineNode` function when you are calculating f, so you really do not need to change much code around. Simply editing the quadtree matrix causes all sorts of cool stuff to happen with the code we were using from Chapter 5. Now go check out demo6_2. The controls are the same as the previous demo except, this time around, more detail is given to areas that are of a higher level of roughness, as you can see from the wireframe in Figure 6.16.

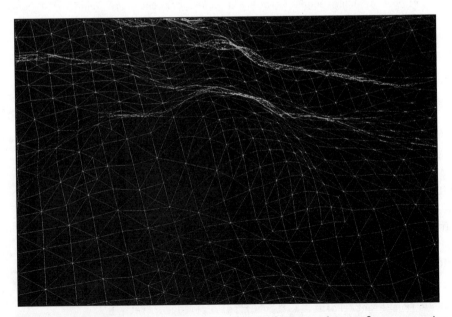

Figure 6.16 *Wireframe screenshot from demo6_2 showing how surface propagation affects the tessellated mesh.*

Speeding Things Up a Bit

The final thing we are going to do is add frustum culling to our implementation, which is a simple way to speed up our implementation. To add frustum culling, the only function we need to edit is RefineNode. Our frustum test is the same thing as Chapter 5. We're going to make a "cube" out of the current node and then test it against the viewport. If the node is in view, we'll continue refining the node. If it's not in view, we'll set the node's quadtree matrix to 0 and eliminate that node and all of its children from the updating and rendering queue.

```
//test the node's bounding box against the view frustum
if( !m_pCamera->CubeFrustumTest( x*m_vecScale[0],
                                 GetScaledHeightAtPoint( x, z ),
                                 z*m_vecScale[2],
                                 iEdgeLength*m_vecScale[0] ) )
{
    //disable this node, and return (since the parent
    //node is disabled, we don't need to waste any CPU
    //cycles by traversing down the tree even further)
    m_ucpQuadMtrx[GetMatrixIndex( ( int )x, ( int )z )]= 0;
    return;
}
```

With that, we end our coverage of the quadtree algorithm and implementation. Check out demo6_3 and witness the result of all of your hard work. Good job!

Summary

It's been a fun chapter, and we covered almost everything to do with Stefan Roetgger's quadtree algorithm. We talked about what a general quadtree is and then discussed all the theory behind the quadtree algorithm. From there, we implemented all the theory. We ended up with a fast, flexible, and good-looking terrain implementation! We have only one more terrain algorithm to cover, so let's get to it!

References

1 Roettger, Stefan, Wolfgang Heidrich, Philipp Slusallek, and Hans-Peter Seidel. *Real-Time Generation of Continuous Levels of Detail for Height Fields.* In V. Skala, editor, Proc. WSCG '98, pages 315–322, 1998. http://wwwvis.informatik.uni-stuttgart.de/~roettger/data/Papers/TERRAIN.PDF.

CHAPTER 7

WHEREVER YOU MAY ROAM

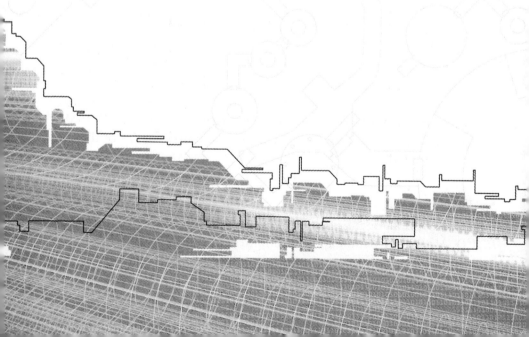

In the final segment of our CLOD terrain algorithm coverage, we are going to cover the Real-Time Optimally Adapting Mesh (ROAM) algorithm. ROAM has been synonymous with terrain for the past few years, but it recently came under fire because it was widely considered "too slow" for modern hardware. By the end of this chapter, you'll be *shocked* that anyone could ever consider it slow! For now, however, let's go over this chapter's agenda:

- Theory behind the ROAM algorithm
- Seamus McNally's ROAM improvements
- ROAM for the new millennium
- Implementing the new and improved ROAM

The agenda might seem fairly routine right now, but it is anything but. We discuss ROAM—the old and new theories—in great lengths, and we also take great care in implementing ROAM so that we can get the most "band for our buck." I'll shut my mouth now so we can get on with the chapter!

The ROAM Algorithm

The ROAM algorithm,[1] developed by Mark Duchaineau, has been *the* standard for terrain implementations over the past few years. ROAM's popularity skyrocketed with the release of Seamus McNally's *TreadMarks*, which implemented some new twists on the classic algorithm's ideas and made people rethink their ideas on what ROAM was. All of this and more are discussed in the first section of this chapter, so let's get going!

Theory

The ROAM algorithm (the whitepaper of which can be found on the CD, Algorithm Whitepapers\roam.pdf) consists of a series of unique ideas that revolutionized terrain visualization. We'll cover the ideas presented in the paper, starting with the base data structure.

The Binary Triangle Tree

The ROAM algorithm uses a unique structure called a *binary triangle tree* to store polygonal information. This tree starts off with a coarse root triangle (see Figure 7.1).

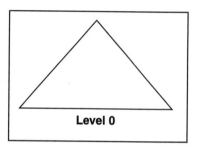

Figure 7.1 *A level 0 tessellation of a Binary Triangle Tree node.*

As trite and coarse as that triangle looks, just remember that it *is* the first level of the tessellation—it's not supposed to be impressive. To traverse down the tree a bit, we want to subdivide the current triangle (level 0 tessellation). To do this, we want to "draw" a straight line from any of the triangle's three vertices that bisects the line, opposite the vertex, into two equal segments, thereby forming two triangles with base angles of 90 degrees. This produces the level 1 tessellation, composed of two triangles (see Figure 7.2).

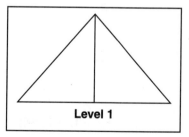

Figure 7.2 *A level 1 tessellation of a Binary Triangle Tree node.*

Wow, an amazing two triangles! We need to make another "subdivision" pass (using the same technique that we did for the previous subdivision).

Doing so produces a level 2 tessellation, taking our triangle count up to 4. (In case you've been sensing a pattern but aren't quite certain about the increase of triangles for every subdivision, I'll just tell you: The number of triangles doubles with each subdivision: 1 (Figure 7.1), 2 (Figure 7.2), 4 (Figure 7.3), 8 (Figure 7.4), 16 (Figure 7.5), and so on.)

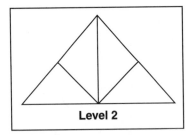

Figure 7.3 *A level 2 tessellation of a Binary Triangle Tree node.*

Here's another subdivision pass, which brings our total triangle count up to 8.

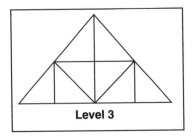

Figure 7.4 *A level 3 tessellation of a Binary Triangle Tree node.*

With Figure 7.5, our total triangle count is up to 16. The subdivisions do not have to stop here; they can continue up until the resolution of the engine's underlying heightmap has been reached. Anyway, the previous tessellation was just to show what a sample tessellation of a single Binary Triangle Tree node would look like. However, contrary to what you might think right now, the actual tree node does *not* contain polygonal information. It simply contains pointers to its neighbors and children, as you'll see a bit later.

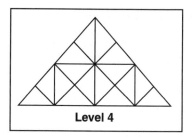

Figure 7.5 *A level 4 tessellation of a Binary Triangle Tree node.*

Tessellating a Series of Binary Triangle Tree Base Nodes

We are going to fill the terrain mesh with several "base nodes" that will link together to form a continuous mesh. As usual, the cracking monster will show its ugly face at one point or another. Therefore, when tessellating (from a coarse level to a more detailed level, similar to the top-down approach we took in Chapter 6, "Climbing the Quadtree"), we might have to "force split" a node or two. Consider the example shown in Figure 7.6.

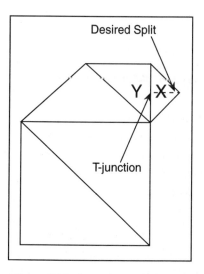

Figure 7.6 *A cracking problem just waiting to happen.*

In Figure 7.6, we want to subdivide triangle X. However, by doing so, we cause a crack by creating a *T-junction*, which is when one triangle is of a higher Level of Detail (LOD) than a neighbor triangle, which is what would happen if we were to subdivide triangle X. (A T-junction would be formed with triangle Y.) To prevent this outcome, we need to *force split* by splitting the other triangles present in Figure 7.6 until they are of a uniform detail level and no T-junctions are present, as shown in Figure 7.7.

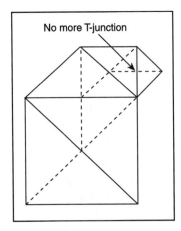

Figure 7.7 *No crack, no T-junction, no problem!*

Splitting, Merging, and an Imaginary Cat

Okay, I'm really not sure how the imaginary cat fits into the equation *throws Mittens off desk.* With the fictitious feline out of our way, we can handle the next—and perhaps most complicated—part of the ROAM whitepaper: splitting and merging. The ROAM paper suggests that instead of starting from scratch every frame, we can base the current frame mesh off of the mesh from the previous frame and add/subtract detail where it is needed.

To accomplish this task, we need to split the triangle tree nodes into two priority queues: a split queue and a merge queue. These queues will keep priorities for every triangle in the tessellated mesh, starting with the coarse tessellation, and then repeatedly force split, or merge, the triangle with the highest priority. It is also important to maintain the requirement that a child node never have a higher priority than its parent.

This is the basic and bare-bones explanation of priority queues because I don't want to spend too much time discussing them at this moment. Just know that priority queues exist and know what basic purpose they serve. We'll come back to them later.

Improvements to the ROAM Algorithm

If you remember our discussion of Seamus McNally's *TreadMarks* from Chapter 1, "The Journey into the Great Outdoors," you'll remember me saying how Seamus really boosted ROAM's popularity with his implementation used in *TreadMarks*. Well, now we're going to get down to the nitty-gritty details about what exactly he changed from the traditional ROAM algorithm. These ideas are also summarized by Bryan Turner in a paper he posted on Gamasutra.[2] You can find the paper and its accompanying demo on the CD in the "Algorithm Whitepapers" directory. Both the demo and paper are compressed into the ROAM_turner.zip file.

Seamus's Changes

Seamus McNally made several highly notable changes to the ROAM algorithm, which you can see in his game *TreadMarks*. The changes that Seamus made sped up the algorithm by decreasing the CPU's workload and using a rather cool trick with the binary triangle tree nodes, also making the algorithm more memory friendly. Following are some of the changes Seamus made:

- No data stored for drawn triangles
- A simpler error metric
- No frame-to-frame coherence

Improving the Binary Triangle Tree Nodes

Instead of storing information for each rendered triangle node, Seamus proposed that each triangle node needs little information to accomplish its task. This information consists of five "links" to triangles related to the current node (see Figure 7.8).

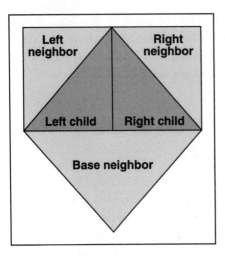

Figure 7.8 *The information that a single Binary Triangle Tree node must contain.*

As you can see, each triangle needs only five links: two links to its children nodes (left and right children) and three to its neighbor nodes (base, left, and right neighbors). Here is some simple pseudo-code for what the structure would look like if you wanted to implement it:

```
Structure BinTriNode {
    BinTriNode* leftChild;
    BinTriNode* rightChild;
    BinTriNode* leftNeighbor;
    BinTriNode* rightNeighbor;
    BinTriNode* baseNeighbor;
}
```

To actually put that structure to use, you can allocate a node pool at initialization that the binary triangle tree can draw triangles from during run-time. This almost eliminates run-time memory allocation for the terrain, and it controls the terrain's level of detail. The terrain then calls upon this node pool for tessellation and rendering, which we'll discuss in more detail soon.

Simplifying the Error Metric

The error metric presented in the ROAM whitepaper consisted of a series of complex mathematical routines (which is why it was not

NOTE

Pre-allocating a memory pool of `BinTriNodes` isn't too hard. You just declare a pointer to a `BinTriNode` buffer (signifying that we'll allocate the buffer later), like this:

```
BinTriNode* pTriPool;
```

Then, to allocate the entire buffer, you use C++'s `new` operator, like this:

```
pTriPool= new BinTriNode[numTris];
```

That's all there is to it! I just thought I'd add that in case you had a question about it.

covered in our brief coverage of the whitepaper). Seamus, however, proposed a much simpler error metric that can be used for detail calculations. (The error metric is used when you're trying to decide whether to split a tri-node and how deeply it should be split.)

The error metric we are going to use consists of a simple calculation and "takes place" entirely on a triangle's hypotenuse. (This calculation should seem familiar to you if you read the geomorphing sections in Chapters 5, "Geomipmapping for the CLOD Impaired," and 6, "Climbing the Quadtree.") We're just going to calculate the delta of the average length and the true length. Consider the triangle in Figure 7.9.

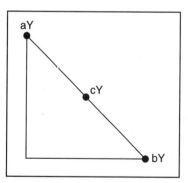

Figure 7.9 *An example triangle for use with the error metric calculation explanation.*

For the calculation, we only need the height components from the marked vertices. We're going to calculate the difference between the approximated values at cY and the actual value, which *is* cY, as shown in Figure 7.10.

$$metric = \left| cY - \frac{aY + bY}{2} \right|$$

Figure 7.10 *The equation to calculate the error metric value for a triangle.*

All we are really doing, as with the geomorphing calculations we discussed in Chapter 5, is trying to figure out how much popping will occur if we subdivide the current triangle. We can determine the amount of popping by first figuring out how large of a change in height will occur if the triangle is subdivided, and then projecting that change to screen pixels. (The latter requires some rather complicated math, and it's really not necessary. All that really needs to be done is calculating the change in world space.)

The Split-Only Method

A few sections ago, we talked about the split/merge ideas presented in the ROAM whitepaper. Seamus proposed that *frame-to-frame coherence* (tessellating the mesh from the previous frame using the split/merge priority queues) should be completely eliminated. Although adding split/merge support (dual-priority queues) can increase the flexibility and speed of your application, it is an advanced topic, and it has a tendency to bog down programmers at times.

What do you do if you don't base the mesh off of the tessellated mesh from the previous frame? Well, you start from a clean slate every frame and implement what is called *split-only tessellation*, which starts at the coarse level 0 detail level and tessellates down to a suitable level of detail. This technique is actually much easier to implement than it sounds.

I will now refer you to Bryan Turner's demo and article on the accompanying CD. Bryan implements many of Seamus McNally's improvements in some easy-to-read code. The CD also includes Bryan's tutorial that his code is based off of. You can find all of this on the CD at Algorithm Whitepapers/ROAM_turner.zip. Check it out!

ROAM 2.0

Yes, that's right: ROAM 2.0. I've been working closely with Mark Duchaineau (creator of the ROAM algorithm) on this chapter so that the text and code will teach you all about the intricacies of the new algorithm which, at the time of writing, has not been published.

We will take this explanation step-by-step, mixing a little bit of theory and implementation into each step. By the end of the steps, we'll have a full ROAM implementation running. Here are the steps we'll take:

1. Implementing the basics
2. Adding frustum culling
3. Adding the backbone data structure
4. Adding split/merge priority queues

Step 1: Implementing the Basics

This step is really just like the title says: *basic*. We don't cover anything complex in this section; we just cover the basics of the ROAM implementation that we are going to code, such as the polygonal tessellation and other fun stuff. Let's get started!

As usual, we are going to split up the implementation into four high-level functions that initialize, update, render, and shut down the engine. For this first implementation, the update/shutdown functions are going to be almost laughably small, consisting of one line each. To stay consistent with previous chapters, let's start with the initialization function and work our way to the shutdown function. However, unlike the previous chapters, I'm going to mix theory with implementation.

Initialization v0.25.0

During initialization, only a few tasks need to be completed. First, it's necessary to quickly describe some details of what the first couple of demos will be like. We will be procedurally generating the terrain on the fly (no heightmaps, no lighting, no cool-looking texture maps, nothing) by using a version of the midpoint displacement algorithm we discussed in Chapter 2, "Terrain 101." This is a simplistic version of midpoint displacement; it can be described in a single mathematical equation, as shown in Figure 7.11.

$$\sum_{l=0}^{levelMax} md_l = \frac{scale}{\sqrt{2^l}}$$

Figure 7.11 *The mathematical equation to calculate the maximum midpoint displacement values for each detail level.*

In the equation, l is the current level (in the loop), and levelMax and md are where we store the scaled (scale) calculations for the current level, l. For those who understand processes better in code form than in mathematical form, here is the code-friendly version:

```
for( lev=0; lev<=levelMax; lev++ )
    MD[lev]= scale/( ( float )sqrt( ( float )( 1<<lev ) ) );
```

We'll be using that table throughout the first few steps of the ROAM implementations, so you'd better start liking it. (CROAM's instance of the table is named m_fpLevelMDSize for the future code samples, just for your information.)

The next segment of code in the book doesn't really relate to the actual ROAM implementation. It just procedurally creates a texture that, when applied to triangles, produces a cool "wireframe-esque" textured mesh.

Update v0.25.0

Okay, I'm not quite sure you can handle this huge function, but I'm going to just tell you about it now and hope that your head won't explode from the immense size of the function when you look at demo7_1's code. The update function, in the case of my implementation, simply contains... an empty function body! Maybe we'll have more to update later on.

Render v0.25.0

The rendering function is split into a subrendering function used for the recursive rendering of subnodes (similar to the RenderNode function in Chapter 6), so the question becomes this: Where do we start? Well, I'll make that question easy for you to answer. (Rather, I'll provide the answer, and you can pretend like you knew it all along.) We'll start with the high-level Render function.

Render

The high-level Render function is rather simple and routine, and it's similar to the high-level Render function from Chapter 6. Most of the work in CROAM::Render is when we try to figure out the root node's vertex information, which consists of a lower-left, lower-right, upper-left, and upper-right vertex. Once that is done, we just need to render the two base triangles using the recursive RenderChild function:

```
RenderSub( 0, verts[0], verts[1], verts[3] );
RenderSub( 0, verts[3], verts[2], verts[0] );
```

You will understand what the arguments to the function mean in just a second, but for now, all you need to know is that we're sending the triangle's vertex information so that the function can either render the triangle or recurse further down and repeat the process for the next triangle.

RenderChild

This function is slightly more involved than the previous functions we've discussed so far, but it's not nearly as complicated as it will be by the time we reach the final step of this implementation.

The function needs to take four arguments, three of which are vertex information and the fourth of which is the current level that is being rendered. (We need the level information so that we can dig into the midpoint displacement table we created earlier.) At the start of the function, we can store the maximum midpoint displacement value for the current level in a local variable, fMD, to make things easier. Then we can calculate the new vertex that was formed when we split the parent triangle (see Figure 7.12).

After this is done, we can do some tricky IEEE floating-point calculations. In a nutshell, IEEE floating-point operations are used to minimize storage and maximize speed for certain variables and certain calculations. In our case, we want to calculate a random perturbation in the new vertex, which was formed from the current triangle's parent's split, height value (Y-component). To do this, we're going to

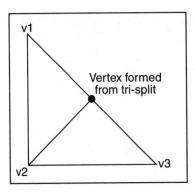

Figure 7.12 *The vertex that was formed from the current triangle's parent's split.*

extract a few values from a hash table filled with random integer variables and fill a local unsigned short variable with that information:

```
pC= ( unsigned char* )fNewVert;
for( i=0, uiS=0; i<8; i++ )
    uiS+= randtab[( i<<8 ) | pC[i]];
```

randtab is the random hash table, and pC is an unsigned char version of the new vertex's information.

After we fill the local unsigned short variable, uiS, with values from our hash table, we need to convert those values to a floating-point value. Using IEEE floating-point tricks to typecast an integer value to a floating-point value is *much* faster than the typical typecasting convention:

```
fFloat= ( float )iInt;
```

However, using IEEE floating-point tricks to typecast an integer variable to a floating-point variable, although faster, is quite a big uglier and incredibly more cryptic to someone who doesn't know what is going on. So, for those who know what is going on, that's great. However, if it confuses you at all, check out the sidebar. (And, for a more rigorous introduction to IEEE floating-point ops, look at gem 2.1 in *Game Programming Gems 2*, which serves as a nice introduction to the topic.)

```
pInt= ( int* )( &fRandHash);


*pInt= 0x40000000+( uiS & 0x007fffff );
fRandHash-= 3.0f;
```

NOTE

This previous IEEE floating point code sample takes the address of the float fRandHash and assigns it to the pointer pInt. If pInt is a 32-bit integer, with 31 being the high bit and 0 the low bit, then we set the 30th bit by assigning it 0x40000000, which gives it an exponent of 128. Then we add the result of the 'and operation' on uiS and 0x007FFFFF.

The 'and operation' is done to mask out any bits that might intrude upon the exponent bits. In the IEEE Floating point standard, the 31st bit is the sign: 0 for positive, 1 for negative. Bits 30–22 are the exponent, and bits 21–0 are the decimal value following the decimal point. So, if uiS contained 0x000F0000 (983,040 in decimal), our floating-point number fRandHash would equal 2.23438, which we then subtract 3 from to get ×1.23438, which in integer format would be 0x40400000.

Basically, all of this is done to speed up lengthy operations, such as type-casting, by using some low-level bit shifting. That's all that there is to it! I hope this little tutorial helps you to understand what exactly is going on.

We want to apply the previous calculations to the new vertex's height value. To do this, we'll use the equation in Figure 7.13.

$$newY = \frac{y1 + y3}{2} + randHash * MD$$

Figure 7.13 *The equation to calculate the new vertex's height value.*

As usual, following is the same equation as in Figure 7.13, except in code form:

```
fNewVert[1]= ( ( fpVert1[1]+fpVert3[1] )/2.0f )+fRandHash*fMD;
```

We need to calculate the distance from the camera's eye position to the new vertex's position. Perform all the steps of the normal distance formula except for the square root step. Leave the value squared. This saves us some valuable processing time by avoiding a call to sqrt. After the distance is calculated, we need to decide whether we want to subdivide the current node. We must meet two requirements to subdivide the node. First, we need to find out if subdividing to another node requires going over the maximum detail level. If it does, then we can't subdivide; we just have to render the current triangle. Second, we need to see if the viewer is close enough to bother with a subdivision. If both of these requirements are met, we can recurse down to the current triangle's two children:

```
//see if we can subdivide the current node or not
if( iLevel<m_iMaxLevel && SQR( fMD )>fDistance*0.00002f )
{
    //render the children
    RenderChild( iLevel+1, fpVert1, fNewVert, fpVert2 );
    RenderChild( iLevel+1, fpVert2, fNewVert, fpVert3 );

    //the current node doesn't need to be rendered
    //because both of its children are
    return;
}
```

Most of the vertex names should be self explanatory. As I said earlier, if the requirements for subdivision are not met, we can just render the current triangle using the three vertices that were passed as function arguments. And that's it for the function!

Shutdown v0.25.0

In the shutdown routine, all we need to do is free the memory that we allocated for the midpoint displacement table. That's all that the shutdown routine requires. Hope you didn't blink!

Demo v0.25.0

Well, we have reached the end of step 1. The end result is rather cool, albeit a bit simplistic. We'll more than make up for this simplicity in the last couple of steps of the implementation, though. For now, go check out demo7_1. The controls are listed in Table 7.1, and a screenshot of demo7_1 (on the CD under Code\Chapter 7\demo7_1) is shown in Figure 7.14.

Table 7.1 Controls for demo 7_1

Key	Function
Escape / q	Quit the program
Up arrow	Move forward
Down arrow	Move backward
Right arrow	Strafe right
Left arrow	Strafe left
+	Increase maximum mesh level
×	Decrease maximum mesh level

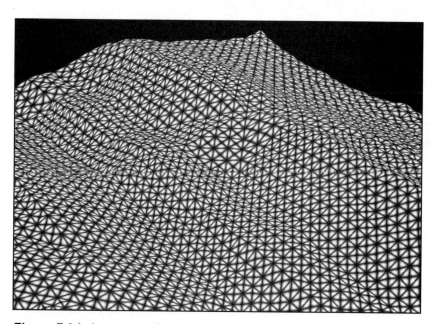

Figure 7.14 *A screenshot from demo7_1, step 1 of the ROAM implementation, which shows the basics of the algorithm.*

It's time to remind you of something. The implementations I'm providing to you on this book's accompanying CD are *only* to give you an idea of how to implement a said technique. They are by no means perfect, highly optimized, or even as highly detailed as they could be. Because the topic of terrain is far from static, the various ways you can implement a certain algorithm can change greatly over time. For the most highly optimized, best looking, and just plain cool implementation of an algorithm, check out my site at http://trent.codershq.com/, where you should find exactly what you're looking for. With that said, let's move on to the next section!

Step 2: Adding Frustum Culling

In this step, we are going to implement frustum culling, which we'll do a bit differently from the way we did it in earlier chapters. We are also going to make the terrain run off of a heightmap (and use texture maps), unlike the last demo. Let's get to it!

Initialization v0.50.0

Initialization is almost the same as it was in Chapter 6 except that we are going to get rid of the procedural grid texture generation. Instead, we are simply going to generate the midpoint displacement size table and then continue on.

Render v0.50.0

Things have changed a bit in the rendering function. Instead of generating vertices for the base triangles in the range of [-1, 1], we are going to be generating them in a rage of [0, size-1], where size is the size of the terrain's underlying heightmap. This is the main step needed to get the engine running off of a heightmap. When this is done, we'll go into our RenderChild routine like the last time.

RenderChild, Revisited

Okay, there have been some changes to this function that will greatly improve the overall performance of our engine and the overall "look" of the rendered mesh. First, let's cover the performance upgrade.

Cull Like You've Never... Oh, Never Mind

When we add frustum culling to this engine, we are doing things a bit differently from the previous two approaches. We are going to use a

bounding sphere to describe the size of our triangle. Then we will test
that sphere against the view frustum for inclusion/exclusion. We need
to know two things for the bounding sphere: its center and its radius
(see Figure 7.15).

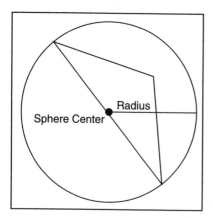

Figure 7.15 *A bounding sphere encasing a single triangle.*

To apply this idea to our code, we need vertex information for the
current triangle. We need to know the three vertices that make up the
triangle. Then we need to calculate the center of the hypotenuse (the
center of the bounding sphere). We will then figure out which vertex
is the farthest from the center— that will be our radius. Here is the
code for one such calculation:

```
fSqrBoundTemp= SQR( ( fpVert2[0]-fNewVert[0] ) )+
               SQR( ( fpVert2[1]-fNewVert[1] ) )+
               SQR( ( fpVert2[2]-fNewVert[2] ) );


//check to see if this is the largest distance
//we've calculated so far
if( fSqrBoundTemp>fSqrBound )
     fSqrBound= fSqrBoundTemp;
```

After we know that, we can easily test for the sphere's inclusion in the
view frustum. If the sphere is included, we can continue on with the
rendering function. If it's not, we can return immediately; if a parent
triangle is not visible, then none of its children, its children's children,
or its children's children's children will be visible. Here is the code for

frustum culling that we'll use for the remaining demos in this chapter. As you can see, it is a *bit* different from the techniques we have been using, but it is also a lot faster. In this code, we are going to test a point against each frustum plane. The second we find out that the point is not inside the frustum, we can quit testing. This technique speeds up our application quite a bit.

```
if( iCull!=CULL_ALLIN )
{
    float r;
    int j, m;

    //perform culling against the view frustum
    for( j=0, m=1; j<6; j++, m<<= 1 )
    {
        if( !( iCull & m ) )
        {
            r= m_pCamera->m_viewFrustum[j][0]*fNewVert[0] +
               m_pCamera->m_viewFrustum[j][1]*fNewVert[1] +
               m_pCamera->m_viewFrustum[j][2]*fNewVert[2] +
               m_pCamera->m_viewFrustum[j][3];

            //check for frustum inclusion
            if( SQR( r )>fSqrBound )
            {
                //check to see if the triangle is actually
                //within the viewing frustum
                if( r<0.0f )
                    return;

                //triangle is within view
                iCull|= m;
            }
        }
    }
}
```

As you have learned in previous chapters, frustum culling speeds up any application, and things don't change here. As a rule, adding frustum culling gives a speed-boost to any application...unless you have a really bloated culling routine.

Texture-Mapping, Detail-Mapping, and a Heightmap

Adding the previously named components to the engine doesn't take much work because we converted the mesh's coordinates to that of the heightmap's. We just need to render everything like we have been in the past few chapters. Bind the textures in the high-level rendering function and calculate the shading/height values for the current vertex. All of this is in demo7_2, so if you're a bit fuzzy on the texture-mapping techniques from the past few chapters, feel free to check it out now. In fact, check out demo7_2 (on the CD under Code\Chapter 7\demo7_2), Table 7.2, and Figures 7.16 and 7.17 anyway.

Table 7.2 Controls for demo 7_2

Key	Function
Escape / q	Quit the program
Up arrow	Move forward
Down arrow	Move backward
Right arrow	Strafe right
Left arrow	Strafe left
+	Increase maximum mesh level
×	Decrease maximum mesh level
T	Toggle texture mapping
D	Toggle detail mapping
W	Render in wireframe mode
S	Render in solid/filled mode

Figure 7.16 *A texture-mapped and detail-mapped screenshot from demo7_2.*

Figure 7.17 *The wireframe version of Figure 7.16.*

Step 3: Adding the Backbone Data Structure

The past few steps have been simple introductions to the fundamental concepts of ROAM 2.0. Now we're going to create the core backbone of what is to come in future steps. Unlike the "old-fashioned" ROAM algorithm, ROAM 2.0 relies on a diamond tree backbone. Although in concept, this is similar to the Binary Triangle Tree that we discussed earlier this chapter, implementing it is rather different. Let's try it!

Diamonds Are a Programmer's Best Friend

The base "unit" for the ROAM 2.0 implementation is called a *diamond*. Each diamond in the tree consists of two right isosceles triangles joined on a common base edge. Each triangle also consists of four child triangles—but we're getting ahead of ourselves a bit. Let's just analyze the base diamond in Figure 7.18.

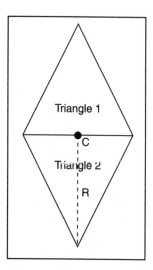

Figure 7.18 *A simple image of the base diamond to be used in the ROAM implementation.*

See? Nothing special. We have a simple diamond composed of two triangles (Triangle 1 and Triangle 2). The diamond's center vertex (C in Figure 7.18) identifies each diamond. Each diamond also contains its squared bounding sphere radius, as we discussed in the previous section, an error metric, its level of resolution (how far down in the diamond tree it is), and its frustum culling bit flag (which we won't need to use until step 4.). Each diamond also contains a series of links, as Figure 7.19 shows.

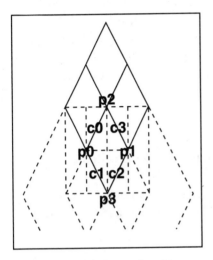

Figure 7.19 *A diamond and its parent/child links.*

As Figure 7.19 shows, the triangle network starts with the same base diamond as that of Figure 7.18, except that we show the two diamonds below it (represented by dotted lines). First, let's start with the children. The children (c0, c1, c2, and c3) are all the children of the original base diamond from Figure 7.18. We then analyze child c1 in more detail, showing its parent links (p0, p1, p2, and p3). Parents p0 and p1 are the left/right parents of the child, and parents p2 and p3 are the up/down "ancestral" parents of the child. This whole diamond concept becomes more obvious as you become more familiar with the whole ROAM 2.0 "system." You can only do that by digging right into the implementation that we will be working on.

The base diamond structure is fairly routine. You already know all of the components that comprise it, so the diamond structure pseudo-code presented next shouldn't come as too big of a surprise:

```
struct ROAMDiamond {
    ROAMDiamond* pParent[4], pChild[4]
    ROAMDiamond* pPrevPDmndnd, *pNextPDmndnd
```

```
       float center[3];
       float bound;
       float error;
       short PQIndex;
       int8 childIndex[2];
       int8 level;

       uint8 cull;
       uint8 flags;
       uint8 lockCount;
       int8 padding[4];
};
```

That's simple enough isn't it? Well, that is the basis for steps 3 and 4 of our ROAM 2.0 implementation, so you better get used to that structure!

Creating a Diamond

Ahhh, if only I could create my own diamonds... Talk about a money maker! Anyway, we're going to be going over some pseudo-code that can "create" the information you need for a new diamond child. This function we are going to discuss is the basis for step 3, so you'd better pay attention!

In the diamond child creation function, the single most important goal we have is for the function to generate the links for the diamond child to keep the mesh consistent. Although step 3 does not provide native crack-fixing support, it is still important to link the mesh's diamonds together. (Link the child to its parents and vice versa.) That's our main goal for the creation function. We also, of course, want to initialize the child's information. After all, what's the point of having a child if it doesn't know anything?

```
ROAMDiamond CreateChild( child, index ) {
    // return if already there
    if (child->pChild[index])
        return child->pChild[index];

    // allocate new one
    k= allocate_diamond();
```

```
    // recursively create other parent to kid i
    if (index<2) {
        px= child->pParent[0];
        ix= (child->childIndex[0]+( index ==0 ? 1 : -1 ) ) & 3;
    } else {
        px= child->pParent[1];
        ix= (child->childIndex[1]+( index ==2 ? 1 : -1 ) ) & 3;
    }
    cx= CreateChild( px, ix );

    //set the child's links
    child->pChild[i]= k;
    ix= ( I & 1 )^1;
    if (cx->pParent[1] == px)
        ix|= 2;
    cx->pChild[ix]= k;

    if (index & 1) {
        k->pParent[0]    = cx;
        k->childIndex[0]= ix;
        k->pParent[1]    = child;
        k->childIndex[1]= index;
    } else {
        k->pParent[0]= child;
        k->childIndex[0]= index;
        k->pParent[1]    = cx;
        k->childIndex[1]= ix;
    }
    k->pParent[2]= child->pParent[index>>1];
    k->pParent[3]= child->pParent[( ( ( index + 1 ) & 2 )>>1 ) + 2];
    ResetChildLinks( );


// compute kid level, vertex position
    k->level = child->level + 1;
    k->center= midpoint( k->pParent[2]->center,
                         k->pParent[3]->center );

    CalculateBoundingRadius( );
```

```
UpdateDmndCullFlags( );

    return k;
}
```

Phew! That's a lot of pseudo-code and a lot of ugly little bit shifting/masking ops! Well, never fear. It's all a lot simpler than it looks. All of the bit shifting and masking is used to figure out a child's orientation in relation to its parent. We could clean all this ugliness up a bit, but by bit shifting instead of dividing/multiplying, we speed things up a bit (not by much, but enough to make a difference in a common-used function). Plus, all these bit ops should make you feel really cool.

Molding the Backbone Diamond Tree Together

Okay, you know most of what you need to know to put step 3 together, but the knowledge you have is slightly fragmented and needs to be "put together." That's the goal of this section, so let's get started!

The Diamond Pool

The diamond pool is a dynamically allocated buffer of diamond structures. This pool is what you "call upon" during run-time when you need a new diamond for the mesh. After you allocate this pool, you need a couple of functions to manage the diamonds that you want to use. For instance, if you would like to create a new diamond, you need to get it from the pool. While you're using that diamond, you don't want to use that *same* diamond somewhere else in your code. It's necessary to create a couple of "security" functions: one function to lock a diamond for use and another function to unlock a diamond from use.

The locking function's job is simply to remove an unlocked diamond from the "free list" of diamonds (the diamond pool). To do this, we need to find the most recently unlocked free diamond (which should be provided as an argument for the locking function), take it for our use, and then relink the old most "recently" unlocked diamond to a different diamond for the next time we want to lock a diamond for use. The unlock function uses a similar methodology, except, well, you do the *opposite* of what was done in the locking function.

We could use one more function to make our life easier, and that would be a diamond creation function, which creates a level of abstraction over the diamond pool. The creation function simply needs to get a pointer to the most recently freed diamond. If there is no diamond to "grab," then we have a slight problem on our hands... Most of the time, though, we don't have to take that into consideration, so don't worry about it too much. Then we want to find out if the diamond has been used before. To do this, we can use one of the diamond structure's member variables as a "been used before" flag. For this, we will use the bounding radius variable. At initialization, we will set this variable to ×1 and, if the diamond is used, it will be set to a different value somewhere along the line. (This value would, most definitely, be above 0—unless, of course, you've seen a sphere that has a negative radius, thereby stretching it into the great unknowns of any 3D coordinate system.) Anyway, if the diamond we're "grabbing" has been used before, we need to reset its primary parent/child links and be sure to unlock its parent diamonds from the pool. We can then continue to lock the grabbed diamond and return the locked pointer to a newly created diamond that we can toy with.

With these pool manipulation functions in place, we have a nice little layer of abstraction over the diamond pool backbone of our ROAM 2.0 implementation. Now we can begin coding a working implementation in step 3 instead of worrying about all this theory and pseudo-code. Hoorah!

Initialization v0.75.0

Step 3's initialization function is quite a bit more complex than in step 2. (Of course, step 2's initialization function was quite simpler than the one presented in step 1, so now you are paying for your "lucky break" in initialization.) We have more "maintenance" to do to get the demo up and running. We have to initialize the diamond pool, take care of two levels' worth of base diamonds (not to mention linking them all together), and a whole bunch of other fun stuff that will boggle your mind. Well... okay, maybe it won't quite *boggle* your mind. In fact, I think I'll even try to make the whole thing easy to learn. Let's go!

First, we need to initialize the memory for the diamond pool. That's not too hard, and I think you can handle it on your own. After that's done, we need to do some "pool cleaning," which is where things might get tricky. To start with, we want to loop through all of the pool diamonds and set the previous/next links to the corresponding diamonds in relation to the current one. See Figure 7.20.

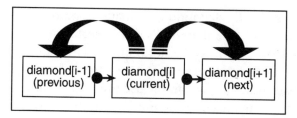

Figure 7.20 *Setting up the diamond pool by linking each node to the previous/next nodes.*

After we've established the links, we can reloop through the pool and initialize the "key" variables for each diamond. The key variables and what needs to be done are as follows:

1. The bounding radius must be set to ×1.0, which marks the diamond node as new. (You can actually use any other floating-point value less than 0. You can even use ×71650.034 if you feel the need.)

2. The diamond's lock count must be set to 0, also marking the node as new and unused.

Next, we must initialize the base diamonds for the mesh. We have two levels of diamonds to initialize: a 3 × 3 level 0 diamond base and a 4 × 4 level 1 diamond base. Both require slightly different computations to figure out the diamond's center, and each requires a different linking technique, but other than that, they basically require the same setup procedure. The diamond's center vertices will be initialized in the range of [×3, 3], so it's important to scale those values according to the size of the heightmap. We also need to calculate the level of the diamond, which isn't as simple as it seems. The base diamonds are rarely involved in the actual rendering process of the mesh, so they actually take a *negative* level. The base diamonds are simply used as a "starting point" for the rest of the mesh. Attempting to render the base diamonds will result in unfortunate errors, and that's never a good thing. After we've taken care of the first part of the base diamond initialization, we need to set the base diamond links, but all of that is fairly routine.

Render v0.75.0

The child-rendering function is almost the same as it was in the previous step, but instead of sending the vertex information for each triangle individually, we are going to send the diamond information and use the vertices contained in the diamond (the diamond's center vertex and the center vertices of its previous and next diamond links). The high-level rendering function has been made even simpler. Instead of calculating the vertices for the base triangles, we simply use the information from the base triangles that we initialized in the initialization function:

```
//render the mesh
RenderChild( m_pLevel1Dmnd[1][2], 0 );
RenderChild( m_pLevel1Dmnd[2][1], 2 );
```

That's all there is to rendering the mesh. We just take the middle two diamonds from the level 1 base diamond set and render their base children. That's all there is to it! Go check out demo7_3 (on the CD under Code\Chapter 7\demo7_3). You won't see much of a visual difference from demo7_2 (as Figure 7.21 will show) because all we did was change the "background" data structures that the engine runs off of. You won't even notice much of a change in speed for the program. This step was mainly to set up the diamond tree backbone that the next two steps will run off of. Anyway, enjoy the demo!

Step 4: Adding a Split/Merge Priority Queue

This is where our implementation gets a *huge* upgrade in speed and infrastructure. Instead of retessellating the mesh after every frame, we will be doing our main tessellation at the beginning of the program and then basing the newly tessellated mesh off of the mesh from the previous frame by splitting/merging diamonds where it is needed. It's important that you understand the diamond backbone structure that we discussed in the previous section before reading this section because this section uses that structure extensively.

The Point of a Priority Queue

You might remember this topic from earlier in the chapter, except then we were talking about triangle binary trees instead of diamonds; however, the basic concepts that we talked about are the same. The priority queue provides a "bucket" for splitting/merging a diamond. The top diamond on the bucket is the diamond with the highest priority, so it will receive the first split/merge treatment. Using these priority

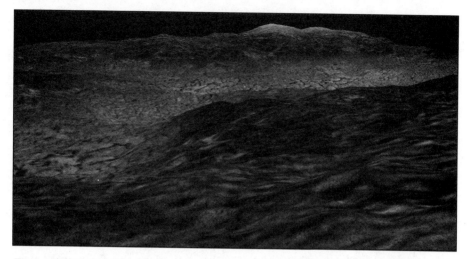

Figure 7.21 *A screenshot from demo7_3, where we added the diamond backbone to the ROAM implementation.*

queues, we aren't forced to reset and retessellate a new mesh for every frame; therefore, we can keep a more rigid polygonal structure, a more consistent framerate, and all sorts of other goodies.

We will implement a dual-priority queue for step 4: one merge queue and one split queue. Splitting a diamond will result in a higher level of detail, and merging a diamond will result in a lower level of detail. By splitting the necessary split/merges into two separate queues, we speed up the process by not having to sort through one mess of split/merge priorities in a single bucket. Now that we know the point of the split/merge priority queue structure, how exactly do we go about implementing it? Well, now is a good time to discuss that!

Implementing the Split/Merge Priority Queue

To begin our split/merge queue implementation, we first need to create two diamond pointer arrays—one array for the split queue and one array for the merge queue. The queues hold diamond pointer information rather than actual diamond data. The engine will use this diamond pointer to access the diamond's information to split or merge it. We are going to give each diamond an index into either the split or merge array to make our life a little bit easier.

First, we're going to need two functions that will update the diamond's priority or the diamond's queue index. We'll discuss the "priority update" function that takes a diamond and updates its priority queue index based on the information for the current viewpoint.

The priority update function takes a diamond pointer and updates its index based on viewpoint-related information (mostly the distance from the diamond's center to the viewpoint and the error metric in relation to the diamond's distance). We want to make sure that this process has not already been done on the diamond by checking a flag somewhere within the structure. Then, considering that this process has not already been performed with the given diamond, we move on to the distance/error calculations. The diamond's error value should have already been calculated when it was created, so that makes our life a bit easier. However, then we need to calculate the diamond's priority based on the projected error value in relation to the diamond's distance from the camera. After this, we need to call the next function to update the priority queue with the diamond's new index and replace the diamond's old index in the queue with its new one. Doing this leads us into the discussion of the second function I was talking about earlier.

The second function, which will be called "Enqueue," is where we update the diamond's entry in its priority queue (either the split queue or the merge queue) by replacing its old entry in the queue with its new entry. (The new entry's location in the priority queue is defined as an argument to the Enqueue function.) As for which queue the diamond is in, that information is provided by one of the flags within the diamond structure, which makes the process even easier! For the first part of this function, we are only concerned with *removing* the diamond from its old position in the queue. When that is done and all the necessary queue flags and links have been resolved, we want to insert the diamond into its new place in the priority queue and update the diamond's flags with the new queue information. (We might actually be moving the diamond from one queue to another, so we might move a diamond that was previously in the split queue to the merge queue, or vice versa.) And that's it! Those two functions are the main diamond manipulation functions to manage the priority queues. The problem is that we are lacking two important functions when it's time to use the diamonds that are present in the split/merge queue: the split function and the merge function.

We will discuss the split function first because it's quite simple. This function takes a diamond pointer as an argument (the diamond pointer is a pointer to the diamond that is to be split) and splits it if it hasn't already been split. To do this, look at the pseudo code that follows:

```
Split( ROAMDiamond* dmnd ) {
    //recursively split parents
    for( int i=0; i<2; i++ ) {
        p= pDmnd->pParent[i];
        Split( p );

        //take p off of the merge queue if pDmnd is its first kid
        if( !( p->splitflags & SPLIT_K ) )
            Enqueue( p, ROAM_UNQ, p->queueIndex );

        p->splitflags|= SPLIT_K0<<pDmnd->i[i];
    }

    //fetch kids, update cull/priority, and put on split queue
    for( i=0; i<4; i++; ) {
        k= GetChild( pDmnd, i );
        UpdateCulling( k );
        UpdatePriority( k );

        //children of the newly split diamond go on the split queue
        Enqueue( k, SPLITQ, k->iq );
        s= ( k->p[1]==pDmnd ? 1 : 0 );
        k->splitflags|= SPLIT_P0<<s;
        Unlock( k );
        UpdateTris( k );
    }
}

    //indicate diamond is split, update queueing, add to checklist
    pDmnd->flags|= SPLIT;
    //freshly split pDmnd goes on mergeq
    Enqueue( pDmnd, MERGEQ, pDmnd->iq );
}
```

The merge function is the split function in reverse. If you understand the split function, you should have no trouble with the merge function!

And that takes care of most of the details of the split/merge priority queue system!

The Triangle System

We are changing around the rendering system quite a bit in this step. Because we aren't completely retessellating the mesh from scratch each frame, we really don't need to update triangle information (the triangles that will be sent to the API, that is) every frame either. We're going to implement a "triangle tree" to keep track of triangles that are on the list to be rendered. This triangle tree is defined by a large floating-point array that serves as a sort of vertex buffer for triangles to be sent to the rendering API. We will store texture coordinates in this array, too. However, to make things easier on us and to clean up the code, we need to come up with manipulation functions to manage the information. We are going to need a function for each of the following tasks:

- "Allocating" a new triangle and adding it to the list
- "Freeing" an allocated triangle from the list
- Adding a new triangle to the list
- Removing a triangle from the list

Remember: We aren't actually allocating/freeing memory in this system— it just *seems* like we are! The allocation/freeing functions are the high-level abstractions that call on the add/remove triangle functions. Let's focus on the low-level manipulation functions because the high-level ones are pretty self explanatory.

The add/remove functions are fairly complementary to each other, so if you understand the workings of one, you will understand the other. (Is it just me, or are there a lot of "opposite" functions in this chapter?) Let's start by covering the triangle adding function. The first thing we want to do in this function is find a free triangle in the array to write to. (This is, essentially, a write-only vertex buffer because we are putting the information in the array and simply sending it off to the API.) After we have a free triangle at our disposal, we can fill its information with the vertex information from the diamond that was passed as an argument to the function. That's all there is to it! We can now move on to implementing step 4.

Initialization v1.00.0

The initialization routine isn't much different from the one in step 3, and the major additions that were made to the function were already talked about when we discussed the split/merge priority queue system. The only other major addition to this procedure is that we must put a top-level diamond on the split queue because all other diamonds come from and grab its triangles to start the triangle-rendering process. To do this, we simply add this code to the end of the initialization function:

```
pDmnd= m_pLevel1Dmnd[1][1];
Enqueue( pDmnd, SPLITQ, IQMAX-1 );
AllocateTri( pDmnd, 0 );
AllocateTri( pDmnd, 1 );
```

That's all that really has been absent from our discussions up to this point. You should have no trouble understanding the rest of the initialization procedure or coding your own from the information presented in this chapter so far.

Update v1.00.0

Gasp! Yes, we *actually* have an update function for this step! This function performs the frame-by-frame updates for the mesh. In this function, we want to update the priority for all queued diamonds, and then we want to do the actual splitting/merging of the diamonds in the priority queues until one of these cases is satisfied:

- The target triangle count has been reached or an accuracy target has been reached.
- We run out of time to split/merge. (We want to limit the amount of splitting/merging done each frame.)
- We run out of free/unlocked diamonds in our diamond pool.

Until one of those cases has been satisfied, we can split/merge to our heart's content! Although we *do* want to keep a nice level of mesh coarseness, we *do not* want too coarse of a mesh. (This is defined by checking "current values" against "maximum values," such as checking the current triangle count against the maximum triangle count.)

Render v1.00.0

Step 4's rendering function is simple. Using the vertex buffer we created earlier, you can easily output all the vertices to be rendered using a single call. The accompanying demo, for instance, outputs all the vertices/texture coordinates as OpenGL dynamic vertex arrays. (For simplicity's sake, I am only using one texture in the demo on the CD and not sending color information.) However, you can port the rendering function to the API of your choice. With that said, demo7_4 is now open for you to check out. You'll notice the largest improvement in this demo if you use a 4096 × 4096 heightmap. Considering that up to this chapter, we've been using 512 × 512 heightmaps, I think it's safe to say that this algorithm is "fairly" powerful. Wouldn't you agree? Check out Figure 7.22 to see demo 7_4 in action (on the CD under Code\Chapter 7\demo7_4).

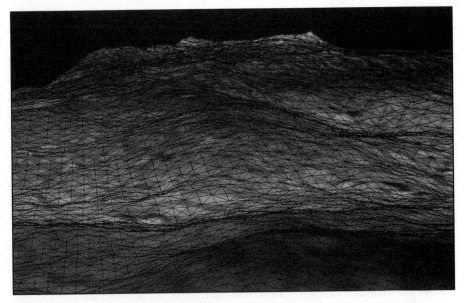

Figure 7.22 *A wireframe render of the mesh from demo7_4 (where we implement dual-priority queues), mixed with a solid render of the mesh.*

If you experiment with demo7_4 a while, you are bound to find a glaring flaw with the mesh (see Figure 7.23). This is because the engine supports a *much* higher level of detail than our heightmap's resolution supports. So, if you can create a large heightmap (8192 × 8192 would probably be a good size) or somehow fractally calculate height values on the fly so that the engine is limited by its allowed LOD and not limited by the heightmap resolution, this "staircase effect" will disappear.

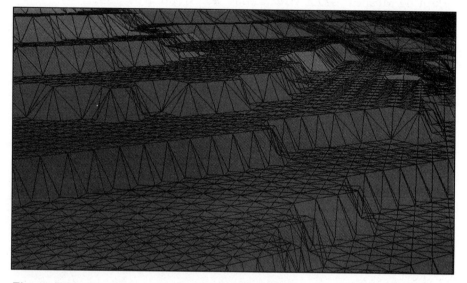

Figure 7.23 *The "staircase" polygon artifact experienced when the ROAM engine's supported detail level surpasses that of the heightmap's.*

Summary

This was the last terrain algorithm chapter for the book… And wow, was it a doozy! In this chapter, we covered lots of ROAM information, starting from the original paper released a few years ago, up to the "new" version of the algorithm. We implemented ROAM 2.0 (the new version of ROAM) in four steps, starting with simple polygonal tessellation and ending with a full-blown and incredibly powerful implementation. The next chapter will be a tremendous journey through a wide variety of tips, speed-ups, and special effects. Get ready!

References

1 Duchaineau, M. et al. "ROAMing Terrain: Real-Time Optimally Adapting Meshes." *IEEE Visualization '97*. 81–88. Nov. 1997. http://www.llnl.gov/graphics/ROAM.

2 Turner, Bryan. "Real-Time Dynamic Level of Detail Terrain Rendering with ROAM." http://www.gamasutra.com/features/20000403/turner_01.htm.

CHAPTER 8

WRAPPING IT UP! SPECIAL EFFECTS AND MORE

We are nearing the end of our journey through the outdoors, so I thought we'd go out in style. In doing so, we're going to do an exhaustive run-through of some of the coolest special effects that programmers have access to with modern hardware. To fit in all the effects possible, I'm going to just give you the agenda for this chapter and get it started. Here's what we'll be talking about:

- Two alternatives for rendering water
- Use of simple primitives to render a scene's surrounding environment
- Camera-terrain collision detection and response
- Two alternatives for rendering fog
- Particle engines and their uses with terrain

That's quite a wide variety of topics we get to talk about. Well, I promise you, each topic will be fun and will open up your options for increasing the realism in an outdoor scene. We'll never get around to discussing them if I keep on talking, though, so let's get going.

It's All in the Water

Water rendering is an important component of any realistic outdoor scene. Sure, some types of scenes—a desert scene, for instance—might have no use for a patch of water, but for most scenes, a little patch of water greatly adds to the mood of the scene. I'm sure the real question on your mind right now is this: "What are we going to be doing?" Well, I'll tell you. We're going to implement two different water algorithms: one simple implementation and one slightly more complex, but infinitely cooler, implementation. Without stalling any longer, let's get started with the simple implementation.

Letting the Water Flow, Part 1

In our first implementation of a water-rendering system, we're going to be relying on a single texture spread across a quad and some simple animation with that texture. Actually, programming this is just about as simple as it sounds, except for one "tricky" problem that will result after we get the system set up right… But, I'm getting ahead of myself; let's take one step at a time.

Let's start off by making a list about what we want our simple water implementation to have:

- The ability to load in a single texture to represent the water's surface
- The ability to render a textured/colored (and alpha-blended) quad

Yup, that's a pretty small list, but don't fear. We will be making lists throughout this chapter, and there will be many larger ones (I know how much you like large lists of requirements for you to comply with). As you can see from the preceding list, we don't have much work to do to get this first demo up and running.

First, we need to discuss how we're going to be rendering this quad that I keep referring to. Look at Figure 8.1, where we have a simple terrain mesh.

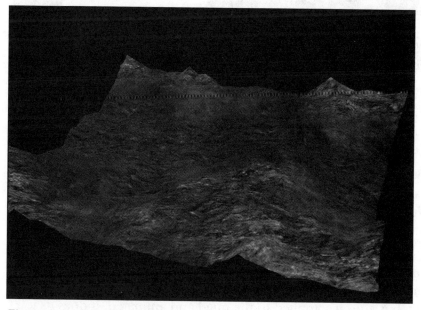

Figure 8.1 *A simple terrain mesh.*

We're going to choose a suitable spot (on the Y axis) for our water patch to inhabit and "slice" a quad through the mesh, as is seen in Figure 8.2.

Figure 8.2 *A simple terrain mesh with a large quad "slicing" it in half.*

That is our beautiful little quad that will soon be our water mesh. It's important to notice the amount of tearing present in Figure 8.2 because we'll be dealing with it in a few paragraphs, but for now, just notice its presence.

Rendering the quad is rather simple. All you need to do is have the user set the center of the quad, get the size of the patch from the user (in world units), and send the vertices to the rendering API. If you seem to be having trouble with this, check out demo8_1/water.cpp on the companion CD.

Our quad is now set up correctly; all we need to do now is add the texture. The texture we're using in the demo (see Figure 8.3) is fairly simple, but after it's applied to the quad and animated, it does its job well.

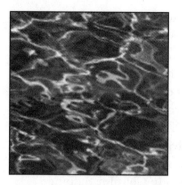

Figure 8.3 *The 256 × 256 water texture used in demo8_1.*

Spreading this single texture across the entire patch (especially because the patch can end up being rather large—the patch in the demo is 1024 × 1024 world units) would result in one ugly water mesh. We want to repeat the texture several times over the mesh, similar to what we did with detail mapping. Next, we can add support for alpha-blending to the mesh (I mean, really, when was the last time you saw an opaque ocean?) to increase the amount of realism. Check out Figure 8.4 to see where we currently stand on our implementation.

Figure 8.4 *The simple water implementation thus far (textured quad and alpha blending).*

We need to add one last thing to our simple water implementation before it is complete. We need to "animate" the texture to make it appear a bit more realistic than a static textured quad. To do this "animating," we are going to have a bit of fun with the texture coordinates that we send to the rendering API. In the accompanying demo, all we are going to do is increase the Y texture coordinate by 0.1f every frame, creating a "flowing water" feel. Overall, it's a pretty cheap way of rendering water, but if you're under a polygon/speed budget, it's a great alternative. And that's it for this simple water implementation. Go check out demo 8_1 (on the CD under Code\Chapter 8\demo8_1), and have some fun with it. Our next water implementation will blow this one of the... well, the water!

Letting the Water Flow, Part 2

Our last water implementation used a total of one primitive composed of two polygons for rendering an entire patch of water. In contrast, the implementation we are about to discuss and implement will be a bit more polygon intensive because our mesh will be made up of a series of uniformly arranged polygons (similar to the polygon arrangement used when we did brute force terrain rendering). By using many polygons, we will be able to create more realistic water, which entails adding waves and a reflection map, instead of the static texture map we used in the previous implementation.

This implementation is a bit more complex than the previous one we just discussed, so let's make yet another list of the things this implementation needs to be able to do and some of the things we need to keep in mind while coding it:

- **A vertex and normal buffer.** Because the water mesh is dynamic, we will want real-time hardware lighting acting on it to make it look realistic.
- **Real-time updating of vertex normals.** That way, realistic lighting (using the API's hardware lighting) can be achieved to add more "depth" to the water.
- **Vertex calculations to create a physically realistic series of waves and ripples.** (It's not technically physically realistic, but it looks that way.)

- **Automatic texture-coordinate generation for the water's reflection map.** That way, the water will look like it is "reflecting" the area around it.

That's the list for this demo. It's twice as large as the previous demo's agenda, but it makes you think what the size of the list will be by the time we reach the twelfth demo in this chapter. (Yes, there are 12 demos for this chapter.) In reality, though, the agendas will be rather short for every demo, but, hey, I have to scare you a little bit!

So, the best place to start is... well, at the beginning. Specifically, we are going to create a highly tessellated mesh of polygons, applying a "reflection map" (see Figure 8.5) and manipulating the mesh's vertices to create a series of waves. While we do this, we want hardware lighting to enhance the realism of the water, so we must dynamically generate vertex normals for the mesh. I know that is all a lot to swallow, but we'll take it step-by-step.

Figure 8.5 *A sample reflection map (also used in demo8_2).*

As you can see from Figure 8.5 (an example of a reflection map, and, coincidentally enough, the same reflection map we will use in our demos for this chapter), a reflection map really isn't anything special. All that a reflection map does is simulate water reflecting the environment around it. This sounds simplistic, but you can do a lot of cool things with it. For instance, you can render your entire scene to a texture every frame (or, at least whenever the viewpoint changes) and use that image as the reflection map for the water. That is just an idea, but it tends to turn out well in implementation. We, however, will not be implementing this cool technique in this book because it isn't a practical real-time technique, but it's something to think about. (And hey, you might even find a demo of it on my site, http://trent.codershq.com/, sometime!) Anyway, back to the topic at hand...

Our vertex buffer will be set up similarly to the brute force terrain engine we worked with in Chapters 2, "Terrain 101," 3, "Texturing Terrain," and 4, "Lighting Terrain." We will lay out the base vertices along the X and Z axes, and we will use the Y axis for variable values (the height values of the vertices). The X/Z values will remain constant throughout the program, unless you want to do something odd, such as stretch your water mesh. Other than that, the values remain constant. To create the water ripples and such, we will be altering only the Y values of the mesh, which leads us into our next topic: altering the Y values of the vertex buffer to create realistic ripples and waves.

For our water mesh, we have several buffers. We've already discussed two of these buffers: the vertex buffer and the normal buffer. However, the one we are going to talk about now is the force buffer. The force buffer contains all the information that represents the amount of external forces acting upon a certain vertex in the vertex buffer. Check out Figure 8.6 for a visual example of what we'll be doing.

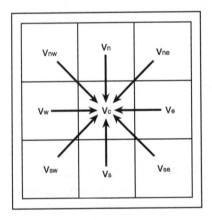

Figure 8.6 *Surrounding forces acting upon the current vertex V_c.*

Figure 8.6 shows how we calculate the force value for the current vertex (V_c in the figure) by taking into account the amount of force that is acting upon the surrounding vertices. For instance, if a vertex V was at rest, and a ripple was caused at a point R, the force of the ripple would eventually meet V. (We want our water to continuously ripple after an initial ripple has been created for our demos, so we are assuming that one ripple will eventually affect every vertex in the mesh.) This causes the vertices around V, especially those in the direction of the ripple, to affect V, and V to continue the ripple's force where the other vertices left off. This is all very fuzzy in text, I know. Figure 8.7 should help you understand.

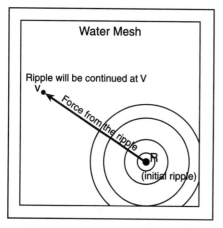

Figure 8.7 *One ripple to bind all the vertices (lame* Lord of the Rings *rip-off).*

Every frame we will be updating the "force buffer," which stores the amount of outside forces acting upon each of the water's vertices. And, for each vertex, we will take into account the force of every vertex surrounding the center vertex (eight vertices). After we fill the force buffer with values, we must apply the force to the vertex buffer and then clear the force buffer for the next frame. (We don't want our forces to stack up frame-by-frame. That would look really odd.) This is shown in the following code snippet:

```
for (x=0; x<m_iNumVertices; x++)
{
    m_pVelArray[x]+= ( m_pForceArray[x]*fDelta );
```

```
m_pVertArray[x][1]+= m_pVelArray[x];

m_pForceArray[x]= 0.0f;
}
```

All we do in this snippet is add the current force (after the time-delta is considered so that frame-rate independent movement can be implemented) to a vertex velocity buffer (used for frame-to-frame vertex speed coherence) and then add that to the vertex's Y value, thereby animating the water buffer. Woohoo! We now have a fully animated water buffer, well, considering that we start an initial ripple somewhere in the mesh:

```
m_pVertArray[rand( )%( SQR( WATER_RESOLUTION ) )][1]= 25.0f;
```

That line starts off a ripple at a random location in the water mesh, with a height of 25 world units. This single line begins all of the animation for our water mesh.

However, before you check out the demo, there is one other thing I must tell you. Even though we have a fully animated water mesh, we are lacking one thing: realistic lighting. We will want to calculate the vertex normals throughout the mesh on a frame-by-frame basis, send the normals to the rendering API, and have the rendering API use those normals to add hardware lighting (per-vertex) into our mesh to increase the realism of our water simulation. Calculating these normals is fairly simple as long as you know your basic 3D theory, but it is of critical importance that you remember to update the normals *every* frame; otherwise, you'll end up with some really flat looking water.

That's it for water! You can check out demo8_2 right now (on the CD under Code\Chapter 8\demo8_2) and zone out witnessing the incredible beauty of our new water rendering system. Also, check out Figure 8.8 to see a static shot from the demo. (Because we've been working on making the water look good in real-time, a static screenshot just doesn't do the effect justice.)

Primitive-Based Environments 101

By now, I'm betting that you're really sick of working on a new terrain implementation, just to see the terrain rendered on top of a black

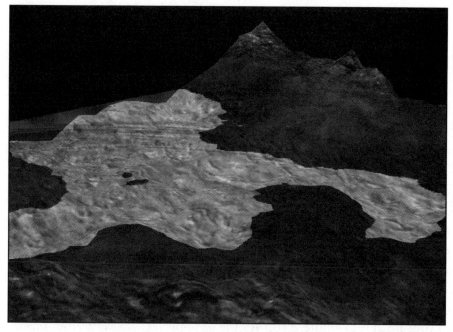

Figure 8.8 *A screenshot from demo8_2, which displays the new water simulation engine.*

background. How boring! Well, now we're going to work on making that black background into a simple environment that is both pretty and speedy. The first type of environment that we will discuss is achieved by using a sky-box. The second type, my personal favorite, is achieved by using a sky-dome. Let's get crackin' on this code!

Thinking Outside of the Sky-Box

The best way to visualize a sky-box is to copy Figure 8.9, cut it out (your copy, not the figure out of the book... you wouldn't want to miss what I have to say on the other side of this page now, would you?), and try to make it into a cube. (You are allowed to use tape for this exercise.) Yep, exactly like you did in elementary school!

This is *exactly* what we are going to be doing in this section. We are going to take six textures and make them into a single cube that will compose the surrounding environment for our outdoor scene. It sounds odd, yes, but it really works. And no, this is not some lame infomercial. Look at Figure 8.9 again, and imagine what it would look like with a series of

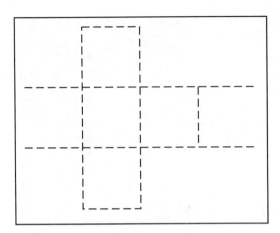

Figure 8.9 *A cutout pattern that can be used to make a simple paper cube.*

textures that blend together seamlessly. (Like magic, I turned that image in your head into Figure 8.10.) It's the semi-perfect answer to the "black screen environment problem" of the demos up to this point.

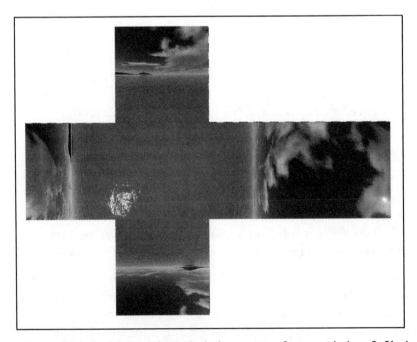

Figure 8.10 *The paper cube, with sky-box textures for use with demo8_3's sky-box.*

Hopefully you were able to construct a paper cube out of the cutout that I provided to you. Now we need to put the sky-box together with code, instead of our hands and tape. This is actually easier than it sounds. We need to load the six textures into our program, construct a simple cube out of six quads, and map our six textures in their corresponding pages.

In our implementation, we want the user to provide the center of the sky-box and its minimum and maximum vertices. (That is all we need to define the cube, as you can see in Figure 8.11.) Other than that, our code can take care of the actual rendering.

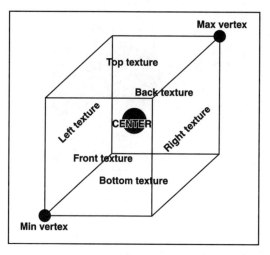

Figure 8.11 *Constructing the sky-box when given its center, a minimum vertex, and a maximum vertex.*

That is all for the sky-box explanation—simple and sweet! If you need to see the specifics of the sky-box rendering, check out skybox.cpp in the demo8_3 directory on the CD (which is under Code\Chapter 8\ demo8_3). Now, look at demo8_3 or Figure 8.12 to see what a sky-box looks like in action. As I said, it's a simple approach to rendering a surrounding environment, but there are several disadvantages to it. First of all, the scene looks slightly out of place unless *the* perfect textures are used for the sky-box. The second problem is that there isn't much room for randomization. Sky-box textures need to be pretty photorealistically accurate to be of much use, so fractal generation is out of the question. In the end, the textures you provide for the sky-box are the ones that will be used every time the program runs. However, in the next two sections, we will learn about a cool alternative to sky-boxes: sky-domes. Let's get to it!

Figure 8.12 *A screenshot showing a sky-box in action.*

Living Under the Sky-Dome

We will be using a sky-dome from this point on in our demos. The real question is this: What is a sky dome? Well, a sky-dome, for our purposes, is a procedurally generated sphere (sliced in half, so we have a half-sphere). To start off, we must discuss how to generate the dome and how to generate texture coordinates for it.

Dome Generation Made Simple

Dome generation is no easy task for someone without a solid math background, so it tends to confuse a lot of people. If you are one of those people, you might want to check out a good sky-dome generation article[1] and use it as a reference to this explanation (which is similar to that of the article, for the theory explanation at least) if it confuses you.

Anyway, to start off the generation discussion, I'll introduce you to the basic equation (see Figure 8.13) that describes a sphere, located at the origin of a 3D coordinate system, with a radius of r.

$$x^2 + y^2 + z^2 = r^2$$

Figure 8.13 *A simple equation that describes an origin-centered sphere for a 3D coordinate system with a radius of r.*

NOTE

To generate a dome, we need to use a lot of the same math that we would use to generate a sphere. (After all, we are basically generating a sphere—just one half of one.) Therefore, a lot of the information in this section will pertain to both dome and sphere generation.

We can derive a simpler equation from the previous one that is better suited to our purpose, as shown in Figure 8.14. This rewrite allows us to calculate the information for a point located on the sphere.

$$f(p_c) = x^2 + y^2 + z^2 - r^2 = 0$$

Figure 8.14 *The equation from 8.13 rewritten so that calculating values for a given point (P_c) is easier.*

However, calculating many points using that equation could prove to be a bit complex. We want to turn our focus to a spherical coordinate system rather than a Cartesian coordinate system, which we've been using up to this point in the generation. With that in mind, we need to rewrite the previous equation and use spherical coordinates, shown in Figure 8.15.

$$p_c = (x, y, z) = f(\Phi, \theta) = (fx(\Phi, \theta), fy(\Phi, \theta), fz(\Phi, \theta))$$

Figure 8.15 *The equation from 8.14 rewritten for use with a spherical coordinate system.*

In the equation, phi (ϕ) and theta (θ) represent the point's latitude and longitude, respectively, on the sphere. In case you don't remember from your middle school days (I know I didn't), latitude represents the lines that run parallel to the earth's equator (they go left/right around a sphere), and longitude runs perpendicular to the equator (up/down). With all of this in mind, we can come up with the final equation that can define the values for any point on our sphere, which can be seen in Figure 8.16.

$$f(\Phi, \theta) = \begin{matrix} fx(r\sin(\Phi)\cos(\theta)) \\ fy(r\sin(\Phi)\sin(\theta)) \\ fz(r\cos(\Phi)) \end{matrix}$$

Figure 8.16 *The final equation that describes any point on a 3D sphere (using a spherical coordinate system).*

That equation can be used to generate an entire sphere, but we only need to generate half of a sphere. We'll deal with that in a few moments, though. Right now, we need to discuss how we are actually going to use the previous equation in our code. First of all, there are a *ton* of points that we can choose to have on a sphere—almost infinitely many. In fact, there probably is an infinite amount of points that we can choose to have on a sphere, but because we have no idea what infinity really is, I tend to stay with the near-infinite answer. Sure, this is a bit fuzzy, but it leaves us more room for being right! Anyway, as I was saying, there is a near-infinite amount of points we can choose for our sphere, so it is natural to assume we're going to have to set up our dome generation function with some sort of resolution boundary; otherwise, we're going to have one really highly tessellated dome.

What exactly do we need to do to generate the sphere, and what do we have to do to limit the sphere's vertex resolution? Well, these two topics go hand-in-hand, so let's discuss them both at once. First, θ can vary from 0 to 2π (which is in radians; in degrees, it can vary from 0° to 359°). In that range, we could find a semi-infinite amount of numbers, so what we want to do is find a nice value to stride through the range.

CAUTION

Be sure when you code your own dome generation implementation (and you are using degrees) that you convert all of your measurements to radians before you send them as arguments to the sin and cos functions because they use radian measurements. This tends to be a huge mistake that is commonly overlooked. Remember: Friends don't let friends send arguments in degrees to C/C++ trigonometric functions.

For instance, let's convert to degrees. In the range of 0° to 360°, we can choose a stride value of 20° and we'll end up with 360°/20° values, or 18 values vertices per column. The smaller stride you choose, the more vertices you'll end up with. We can do the same thing with the ϕ values. Now we need to convert the previous text into code, which, surprisingly is a lot easier to understand than the text.

```
for( int phi= 0; phi <= ( 90-phiStride ); phi+= phiStride )
{
    for( int theta= 0; theta <= ( 90-thetaStride ); theta+= thetaStride )
    {
        //compute the vertex at phi, theta
        vertexBuffer.x= radius*sin( phi )*cosf( theta );
        vertexBuffer.y= radius*sin( phi )*sinf( theta );
        vertexBuffer.z= radius*cos( phi );
    }
}
```

See how simple that is? Well, that's all you really need to do to generate the vertices for the dome; however, now we need to organize those vertices into a triangle strip. That means that during generation, we make a triangle out of each individual vertex (by connecting that vertex to two surrounding vertices) and then compute texture coordinates.

This is quite a bit simpler than it sounds. If you have a question or two, take a look at the code in skydome.cpp in the demo8_4 directory on the CD.

Rendering the Sky-Dome

Generating the sky-dome mesh is the hardest part. Now we just need to sit back and send the vertex buffer to the rendering API. First, though, I want to discuss what kind of texture we want to use to texture the sky-dome. The cool part about using a sky-dome is that you don't need a bunch of textures to make it look good; you simply need one! For instance, in demo8_4, we use the texture that is shown Figure 8.17.

Figure 8.17 *The texture that is used for the sky-dome in demo8_4.*

Now check out demo8_4 and take a look at the rendering code. It's all simple; we just send the vertex and texture buffer to the render API and they are rendered as our beautiful sky-dome. You can find demo8_4 on the CD under Code\Chapter 8\demo8_3. Enjoy the demo and the screenshot from that demo shown in Figure 8.18.

Fractally Generating a Cloud Texture

We don't always have to use a static texture for our sky-domes; we can also generate our own cloud texture fractally as a preprocessing step for our program. This is a cool thing to do because it adds more randomization to your program (which is always fun because people tend to get sick of redundant textures). However, we will not be using the

Figure 8.18 *A screenshot from demo8_4, where we implement a sky-dome and apply a cloud texture to it.*

fractal generation techniques that we discussed in Chapter 2; we will be using a new algorithm for fractal generation. If you understood the fractal generation algorithms presented in Chapter 2, this section should be a breeze.

Fractal Brownian Motion Fractal Theory

In this section, we are going to discuss *Fractal Brownian Motion* (FBM) fractals[2]. These are fractals that encase a combination of unique noise functions. We will discuss two types of noise: white noise and pink noise. White noise is random and sporadic, sort of like what you see when you turn on your TV to a channel that your antenna/satellite doesn't receive, and you get that static screen with the annoying sound. Pink noise is like "uniform noise"; it puts a limit on how the values change from one point to another.

To create pink noise, you create a regular array of values, iterate through the array, and store random values in every spot. After that is done, reiterate through them and interpolate the values to smooth them out; then make the noise a bit more coherent and smooth.

Perlin Noise

Ken Perlin was the first person to use pink noise for computer graphics when he created his now-infamous noise( ) function. He even won an Academy Award for it. This type of noise is now called *Perlin Noise.*

Ken Perlin's home page (http://mrl.nyu.edu/~perlin/) has the following cool little code snippet, which you can paste into your compiler and compile to create a nifty little console program:

```
main(k){float i,j,r,x,y=-16;while(puts(""),y++<15)for(x
=0;x++<84;putchar(" .:-;!/>)|&IH%*#"[k&15]))for(i=k=r=0;
j=r*r-i*i-2+x/25,i=2*r*i+y/10,j*j+i*i<11&&k++<111;r=j);}
```

Check it out. It's a neat snippet, and it's well worth the 2 minutes it takes to get the program running.

There is also a value called *frequency,* which can be used to control the randomness of the noise. The higher the frequency, the more randomness that occurs. (It becomes more like white noise.)

After you have created some pink noise, it is easy to start creating the FBM fractal by combining or multiplying the results from other noise functions. However, before we get much further, it is important to note that you can use other values to control the noise that is generated. We have already mentioned frequency, but you can also use octave, amplitude, and H parameters. The *octave* value sets how many noise values are added or multiplied together. The *amplitude* value adjusts how high the noise values are (or, if we are using the fractal generation for a heightmap, it increases the average height of the generated values). And the *H parameter* controls how much the amplitude changes for each octave. And that just about wraps up the theory for this fractal generation algorithm. Now it's time to implement it!

Implementing Fractal Brownian Motion for Cloud Generation

To start off, we're going to create a function to get a random value in a range of numbers, which we did in Chapter 2, "Terrain 101," when we did our two examples of fractal height map generation. This time, however, we're putting a slight twist on the function. Here it is:

```
float CSKYDOME::RangedRandom( int x, int y )
{
    float fValue;
    int n= x+y*57;

    n= ( n<<13 )^n;

    fValue= ( 1-( ( n*( n*n*15731+789221 )+1376312589 ) &
            2147483647 )/1073741824.0f );
    return fValue;
}
```

That is our ranged random function. All it does is find a random value in a range of numbers; for instance, it will find a random value between 1 and 77. That is the basis for our FBM implementation. We're also going to make a variation of that function, called `RangedSmoothRandom`, which creates a more uniform random value than the `RangedRandom` function.

We also need a function to interpolate two values after we're given an interpolation bias. This function is called `CosineInterpolation`, and we'll use it in conjunction with the `RangedSmoothRandom` function to form the basis of our noise generation.

Now for the actual noise generation function. What we are going to do is calculate a series of random values using the `RangedSmoothRandom` function. Then we'll interpolate them using the `CosineInterpolation` function. Here is the function:

```
float CSKYDOME::Noise( float x, float y )
{
    int iX= ( int )x;
    int iY= ( int )y;
    float f1, f2, f3, f4, fI1, fI2, fValue;
    float fFracX= x-iX;
    float fFracY= y-iY;
```

```
    //generate a random noise value
    f1= RangedSmoothRandom( iX,   iY );
    f2= RangedSmoothRandom( iX+1, iY );
    f3= RangedSmoothRandom( iX,   iY+1 );
    f4= RangedSmoothRandom( iX+1, iY+1 );
    fI1= CosineInterpolation( f1, f2, fFracX );
    fI2= CosineInterpolation( f3, f4, fFracX );
    fValue= CosineInterpolation( fI1, fI2, fFracY );
    return fValue;
}
```

As you can see, first we get the random value for the current point in question; then we get values from three surrounding points. Next, we want to interpolate the values from the first two random calculations, interpolate the values from the third and fourth calculations, and interpolate the two interpolate values. BAM! We have our noise value for that point. This function on its own will not do much, so we need to create a function to create an entire FBM fractal.

Creating an FBM fractal value, now that we have the necessary base functions, is actually quite easy. The fractal creation function needs to take arguments for all of the values we discussed earlier: octaves, amplitude, frequency, and H. We also want to take an (x, y) coordinate set so that we can calculate the FBM value at a specific point. Here is the FBM function:

```
float CSKYDOME::FBM( float x, float y, float fOctaves,
                     float fAmplitude, float fFrequency, float fH )
{
    float fValue= 0;

    //generate a fractal value using "fractal brownian motion"
    for( int i=0; i<( fOctaves-1 ); i++ )
    {
        fValue+= ( Noise( x*fFrequency, y*fFrequency )*fAmplitude );
        fAmplitude*= fH;
    }

    return fValue;
}
```

See, I told you it wasn't hard! That is our entire FBM generation system, but it isn't enough to actually create our cloud texture yet. Now we need to work on the cloud generation function. The cloud generation function still needs to obtain octave, amplitude, frequency, and h information for fractal generation, but it also needs to take a size argument (how big we want our cloud texture map to be), and a blur argument. (The generated fractal won't be fuzzy enough to pass as a bunch of clouds, so we are going to want to blur it a bit.) To create the fractal data buffer, we need to do this:

```
for( y=0; y<size; y++ )
{
    for( x=0; x<size; x++ )
        fpData[( y*size )+x]= FBM( ( float )x, ( float )y, fOctaves,
                                    fAmplitude, fFrequency, fH );
}
```

That will create the entire FBM fractal for us; however, we need to do a bit more than that to create a decent cloud texture. The generated fractal will contain a lot of noise, so we want to choose a cutoff height and eliminate all the values that are below that height (thereby turning them black, instead of a shade of gray). We will then replace the black with a blue and pass a blur filter over the entire field. Then we'll send the data to the rendering API and turn it into a texture. And that's it! We now have a fractally generated cloud texture! Check out demo8_5 on the CD (under Code\Chapter 8\demo8_5) and Figure 8.19 to see a screenshot from that demo.

Camera-Terrain Collision Detection and Simple Response

Do not let the heading fool you; this section is actually incredibly simple and short, but I'm betting that you're sick of having the camera pass right through solid terrain, so we're going to implement some simple collision detection. Look at Figure 8.20 to see exactly what we need to do.

Figure 8.19 *A screenshot from demo8_5, which implements a fractal cloud texture generation system and uses the texture on a sky-dome.*

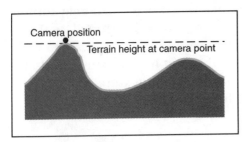

Figure 8.20 *Sample camera-terrain collision. The camera, at its current spot, must be prevented from crossing the dotted line, which means that the camera will not pass through the terrain at its current point.*

We must implement what the figure shows into our code. Doing this takes about six lines of simple code. First, I want to add boundaries around the terrain mesh so that the camera will not go outside of the mesh's area any more. We are going to clamp the camera's position to [0, size of terrain mesh] to accomplish that. Then we want to test the camera's Y coordinate against the terrain mesh's height at the camera's (x, z) position.

```
ucHeight= g_ROAM.GetTrueHeightAtPoint( g_camera.m_vecEyePos[0],
                                       g_camera.m_vecEyePos[2] );

if( g_camera.m_vecEyePos[1]<( ucHeight+5 ) )
    g_camera.m_vecEyePos[1]= ucHeight+5;
```

That is the entire collision detection and response code. (I also gave the camera a "free buffer" of about 5 pixels so that our near-clipping plane doesn't interfere with the terrain.) If our camera is lower than the terrain's height at that point, then we set the camera's height to the terrain's, which prevents the camera from going any lower and passing through the terrain. That's it for this little tip. Check out demo8_6 on the CD, under Code\Chapter 8\demo8_6.

Lost in the Fog

In this section, we're going to implement two types of fog: distance-based fog and vertex-based fog. Both of these types of fog have hardware support, so it's not really a complex topic. It's more of a how-to guide for using the fog correctly and showing some cool things that can be done with it. Let's get started with the distance-based fog explanation.

Distance-Based Fog

Distance-based fog is always based on the viewpoint. All you have to do to use it is pass the starting depth and the ending depth to the hardware API and then do anything else you want to customize the fog (color, density, and so on). This is far from a complex discussion, but getting the fog to look right takes a bit of understanding of the system; otherwise, you'll end up with some really screwy-looking fog in your scene. Look at Figure 8.21 to see how the fog will work.

As the figure shows, the start depth controls the fog's entry point into the scene. Then the fog becomes progressively denser (based on the density that you pass to the rendering API) until it reaches the end depth, where it ceases to exist.

Distance-based fog is great for covering up LOD changes in the distance or for covering up a low LOD. It's also effective if you want to reduce the polygon count by eliminating objects in the distance and you would like the fog to cover that up. This fog is also decent at setting

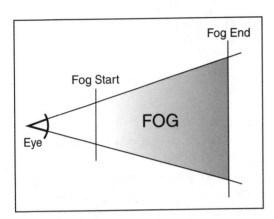

Figure 8.21 *How distance-based fog will work.*
It starts at a start depth and gets progressively denser
until it reaches the end depth.

the mood for the demo. For the most part, however, distance-based fog isn't the best alternative as far as fog implementations go. Nonetheless, it's a fairly cool and simple-to-implement effect; with that said, check out demo8_7 on the CD under Code\Chapter 8\demo8_7 and the now-routine screenshot of the demo in Figure 8.22.

Figure 8.22 *A screenshot from demo8_7, where distance-based fog is implemented.*

Vertex-Based Fog

Vertex-based fog is used completely differently from distance-based fog. When you specify a starting/ending depth, it now applies to the Y axis instead of the Z axis. You are also providing fog coordinates for the current vertices that are being rendered. (By the way, all of this is accessible via the OpenGL extension "GL_FOG_COORDINATE_EXT," which is what is used in this section's accompanying demo.) Vertex-based fog, sometimes called volumetric fog, is also not view-dependent. After you provide coordinates and a starting/ending height, the fog stays at that location throughout your program, which makes it ideal for a couple of cool effects, such as creating mist rising from our water patch.

In fact, creating mist rising from our water patch sounds like a decent idea, so let's continue with the previous train of thought. What we want to do is provide a decent starting/ending height so that our mist will rise to an appropriate height level. You'll want to check out the source for this demo because a lot of the code is API-specific, but I thought I'd give you an idea of what this effect can accomplish.

I provided two demos for this effect to show just what you can do with it. The first demo, demo8_8a, shows some simple gray mist rising from our water. (You can adjust how low/high the fog rises by using the +/- keys.) The second demo, demo8_8b, is based on a dark scene and has a blue mist rising from the water, making the water seem illuminated. I think you'll like both demos. Check them out, and take a look at Figure 8.23.

Figure 8.23 *Screenshots from demo8_8a (left) and demo8_8b (right), which show vertex-based fog.*

Particle Engines and Their Outdoor Applications

I know, I know. You must be asking yourself, "What do particle engines have to do with an outdoor scene?" Well, actually, quite a lot. Particle engines are great to use for rendering rain, snow, comets falling from the sky, and gaping craters in the terrain surface. (You might find a demo exactly like that on my site, if you know what I mean.) Before we can get to the really cool stuff, though, we need to spend a few pages on particle theory... mostly because I have an odd obsession with particle engines, but also because I think the theory will be useful for you.

Particle Engines: The Basics

In case you aren't familiar with particles engines (in which case you wouldn't quite understand this section's introduction, so you might want to reread it after you understand what a particle engine is), I'll give you a quick intro. William T. Reeves developed particles engines in 1982. Reeves was searching for a way to render "fuzzy" objects, such as fire and explosions, dynamically. (Particle engines are a pyromaniac's best friend.) Reeves came up with a list of requirements to implement such a "fuzzy" rendering system:

- New particles must be generated and placed into the current particle engine.
- Each new particle must be assigned its own unique attributes.
- Any particles that have outlasted their lifespan must be declared "dead."
- The current particles must be moved according to their scripts.
- The current "alive" particles must be rendered.

I hope you were paying attention because we will be implementing everything on that list! That doesn't really help you to understand what a particle engine is, though. Basically, a *particle engine* is a "manager" of one or more particle systems. A *particle system* is a manager of several individual particles (which can be points, lines, 3D models, or anything else) that a particle emitter (which shares the properties of a base particle system) creates. See this relationship visually in Figure 8.24.

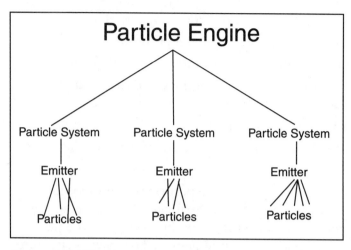

Figure 8.24 *Visual explanation of the relationships in a particle engine.*

Figure 8.24 represents what would be featured in a full, complex particle engine, but we're going to stick to the basics for this section because we don't need all the advanced functionality. However, if you would like to see a complex particle engine, check out my site at http://trent.codershq.com, where you can find the code for a rather complex engine.

Anyway, here's a quick little "particle timeline" for a single particle. The particle is created by iterating through a statically allocated buffer and looking for an "open spot" (marked by a "dead" flag) where we can place the new particle. This particle will take on the default properties of the particle system, and the particle will follow a trajectory until its life counter hits zero. Then the particle will be marked as "dead," and the whole process will start all over. That is the lifetime of a single particle. We're likely to have about 10,000 of these flying around the screen.

Of course, a particle is more than just a speck; it has quite a bit of information that you can use to create almost any special effect imaginable. Here are the properties that a typical particle needs to have:

- **Life span.** This is how long the particle will live.
- **Current Position.** This is the particle's current position in 2D/3D space.

- **Velocity.** This is the particle's direction and speed.
- **Mass.** This is used to accurately model particle motion.
- **Color.** This is the current color of the particle (RGB triplet).
- **Translucency.** This is the current alpha value (transparency) of the particle.
- **Size.** This is the particle's visual size.
- **Air Resistance.** This is the particle's susceptibility to friction in the air.

With that in mind, we can create a simple particle structure for use with our particle engine. Remember: We are greatly simplifying the whole particle engine architecture discussed earlier by cutting out the particle system and complex particle emitter middlemen. The particle structure that follows looks similar to the one we'll be using for our demos.

```
struct SPARTICLE
{
    float m_fLife;

    CVECTOR m_vecPosition;
    CVECTOR m_vecVelocity;

    float m_fMass;
    float m_fSize;

    CVECTOR m_vecColor;
    float m_fTranslucency;

    float m_fFriction;
};
```

As you can see, we implemented all of the requirements in our previous particle-attribute list into our particle structure. How are we going to use this? Well, I'll show you, but first let me demonstrate the particle engine class because it will be easier to understand everything if I show you this first:

```
class CPARTICLE_ENGINE
{
```

```
     private:
          SPARTICLE* m_pParticles;
          int m_iNumParticles;

          int m_iNumParticlesOnScreen;

          //gravity
          CVECTOR m_vecForces;

          //base particle attributes
          float m_fLife;

          CVECTOR m_vecPosition;

          float m_fMass;
          float m_fSize;

          CVECTOR m_vecColor;

          float m_fFriction;

     void CreateParticle( float fVelX, float fVelY, float fVelZ );

     public:

     CPARTICLE_ENGINE( void )
     { }
     ~CPARTICLE_ENGINE( void )
     { }
};
```

That is our engine structure as it stands now (minus the member customization functions, but those are all one line "Set____" functions that you've seen before, namely in the CTERRAIN class). As you can see, this structure has a lot of the same variables that our particle structure has. These are the "parent" or the default values that we are going to give each particle upon initialization. We also have a potential particle buffer (which will be created in the initialization function, as is now a routine aspect for our code). I want to concentrate on the CreateParticle right now because it is an integral part of our engine.

The CreateParticle function implements the "life of a particle" segment that we talked about earlier. It loops through the engine's entire particle buffer, finds a "dead" particle, and then uses that free space to create a new particle based on the default values that the engine provides. It's a pretty simple function, so you could probably code it easily yourself. If you're having a hard time, check out particle.cpp under the demo8_9 directory on the CD.

The other function I want to discuss is the engine's Update function. Understanding its simplistic form is important if you want to understand the more complex form of it in the third demo. This function iterates through the entire particle buffer, moves the particle based on its current velocity, and reduces/increases the velocity due to air resistance/friction and the external forces acting upon the particle (gravity, wind, and so on). We also increase the translucency for the particle as the particle ages and gets closer to death. You can see all this in the code snippet that follows:

```
void CPARTICLE_ENGINE::Update( void )
{
    CVECTOR vecMomentum;
    int i;

    //loop through the particles
    for( i=0; i<m_iNumParticles; i++ )
    {
        //age the particle
        m_pParticles[i].m_fLife-= 1;

        //only update the particle if it's alive
        if( m_pParticles[i].m_fLife>0.0f )
        {
            vecMomentum= m_pParticles[i].m_vecVelocity *
                         m_pParticles[i].m_fMass;

            //update the particle's position
            m_pParticles[i].m_vecPosition+= vecMomentum;

            //set the particle's transparency (based on its age)
            m_pParticles[i].m_fTranslucency= m_pParticles[i].m_fLife /
                                             m_fLife;
```

```
                //now it's time for the external forces to take their toll
                m_pParticles[i].m_vecVelocity*= 1-
m_pParticles[i].m_fFriction;
                m_pParticles[i].m_vecVelocity+= m_vecForces;
        }
    }
}
```

That about wraps it up for the first demo. All the initialization and shutdown functions are similar to what you've seen in previous demos, so you should have no problems in understanding them. And the rendering function is pretty simple right now. I wanted to stick to the basics for the first demo, so the demo just renders simple alpha-blended pixels. Check out the demo, demo8_9 (on the CD under Code\Chapter 8\demo8_9), and also look at the controls for the demo (see Table 8.1). For what might be the first time in this entire book, I am not showing a screenshot for this demo; viewing a screenshot of non-moving pixels is not that interesting. However, the demo is pretty cool.

Table 8.1 Controls for demo8_9

Key	Function
Escape / Q	Quit the program
W	Render in wireframe mode
S	Render in solid/fill mode
E	Create a particle explosion

Taking Particles to a New Dimension

Well, we're only *sort of* taking particles to a new dimension; in the previous demo, we were using pixels, and now we'll be using a 2D texture. However, with using textures comes a rather serious, new problem. We are doing particles in a 3D world, and because the particles are based off of a 2D texture, this means that one dimension is not defined. Therefore, as a viewer walks around particles, he will see the textures getting "flat." This is unacceptable, so we need to implement something called billboarding.

Billboarding

Billboarding is when you need to alter the orientation of a two-dimensional object (such as a quad) so that it will face the user. To do this, you need to extract the current matrix from the rendering API and find the "up" and "right" vectors based on that matrix. That might not mean much to you, so let me elaborate a bit. When you extract the matrix from the API, you can put it in an array of 16-floating point values. (This is how OpenGL executes this for a 4×4 matrix). After you have the array populated with values from the matrix, you can extract the information for the up and right vectors, like what is shown in Figure 8.25.

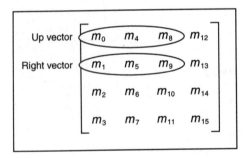

Figure 8.25 *How to extract the information for the up and right vectors from a 4×4 matrix.*

Now we need to apply that to our quad-rendering code:

```
QuadTopRight= ( ( RightVector+UpVector )    *
                  ParticleSize )+ParticlePosition;
QuadTopLeft= ( ( UpVector-RightVector )*
                  ParticleSize )+ParticlePosition;
QuadBottomRight= ( ( RightVector-UpVector )    *
                    ParticleSize )+ParticlePosition;
QuadBottomLeft= ( ( RightVector+UpVector ) *
                  -ParticleSize )+ParticlePosition;
```

Then you send those vertices to the rendering API (with texture coordinates, of course), and BAM! You now have billboarded particles! Take a look at demo8_10 (on the CD under Code\Chapter 8\demo8_10), and check out Figure 8.26. See how much texturing can add to the simulation?

Figure 8.26 *A screenshot from demo8_10.*

Adding Data Interpolation

The last main change we're going to do to our particle engine is data interpolation. This is a great addition to our particle engine because it allows us to make every effect we desire a lot more realistic than it would've been using the engine in the previous section. Data interpolation, as you know from the "Fractal Brownian Motion Fractal Theory" section, is when we interpolate two pieces of data given a bias. For our particle engine, we are going to use linear interpolation, but it is possible to add quadratic interpolation for an even cooler effect.

Our particle engine, instead of keeping track of a single default value for a certain particle property, now keeps track of a default starting value and a default ending value. We're also adding "interpolation counters" for all of our particle properties. This counter is calculated after a particle is created and will be used to increase/decrease the values of a current particle property. Here is how we'll calculate the counter for, say, a particle's size:

```
particles[i].m_vecSize= m_vecStartSize;
particles[i].m_vecSizeCounter= ( m_vecEndSize-particles[i].m_vecSize ) /
                                  particles[i].m_fLife;
```

That is how we'd start off the particle and its data. Every frame, we'd do this:

```
particles[i].m_vecSize+= particles[i].m_vecSizeCounter;
```

That's all there is to it. Of course, you'd have to apply these concepts to every particle property, but you get the jist of it. Feel free to check out demo8_11 on the CD under Code\Chapter 8\demo8_11, which is slightly different from the previous couple of particle demos, as you'll see in Figure 8.27.

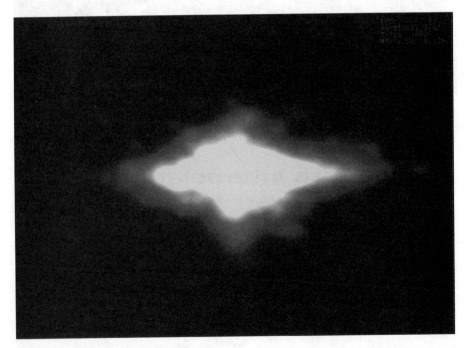

Figure 8.27 *A screenshot from demo8_11.*

Applying a Particle Engine to an Outdoor Scene

Now, for the final demo in this chapter, we are going to apply a particle engine to an outdoor scene. To do this, we are going to create rain. You have several options for doing this, but the way we are going to do it is by creating an imaginary cube around the camera's eye position. Then we'll populate that cube with raindrops at the max height, at a random (x, z) coordinate.

You might be thinking that we need a special texture to create a rain particle, but this is not the case. All we need to do is scale the X coordinate of our particle size down a bit, which makes our old flare-texture into something that resembles a raindrop (see Figure 8.28).

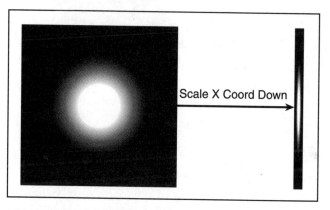

Scale X Coord Down

Figure 8.28 *Scaling the particle "flare" texture down on the X axis to create a raindrop like texture.*

The only unrealistic part of our "rain cube" approach is that it does not check for collision with the terrain, which tends to produce an odd-looking effect when the camera is pressed up against a mountain; yet the viewer can still see rain in the distance. This is fairly easily cured by adding collision detection to the particle engine, but that is a task I leave to you. Go treat yourself to this book's final demo, demo8_12 on the CD under Code\Chapter 8\demo8_12, as well as Figure 8.29, the screenshot of that demo.

Figure 8.29 *A screenshot of demo8_12, the book's final demo, where a particle engine is used to create real-time weather (rain).*

Summary

This chapter was a vicious run-through of a large amount of special effects and tips. We covered water, rendering of environments with sky-boxes and sky-domes, camera-terrain collision detection, fog, and how particle engines can be applied to outdoor scenes. This is also the final chapter in the book, so unfortunately, it's time to wrap everything up.

Epilogue

Wow! To think that this is already the end. Well, to tell you the truth, it feels like the end, and I'm ready for a nice long break (a whole two days or so). Although this book is rather small compared to a lot of programming books on the market these days, let me tell you, a lot of work went into this little guy. I did my best to make sure that all the information in this book is completely correct, and I even had the authors of the three main terrain algorithms (de Boer's geomipmapping algorithm, Rottger's quadtree algorithm, and Duchaineau's

ROAM algorithm) review the chapters to make sure that the information was correct. It is my hope that you enjoyed the book, but before I say goodbye permanently, let me refer you, yet again, to some good terrain information sites.

As I mentioned in Chapter 1, "The Journey into the Great Outdoors," the Virtual Terrain Project is one of the Internet's leading sources of terrain information, and it can be found at http://www.vterrain.org/. GameDev.net (http://www.gamedev.net) has a couple good terrain articles, but, more importantly, it has a good forum where you can post any terrain issues/questions that you might have. Flipcode (http://www.flipcode.com) also has some helpful terrain tutorials that you can look up; after you get your "1337" terrain engine up and running, you can submit it as an "image of the day" to them!

And, with that, this book comes to an end. Be sure to check out the accompanying CD (and the appendix, which covers it) as well as the sites I listed previously. And, for my final note in this book, don't let a set implementation limit your imagination; always strive for innovation over imitation. With that said, I'm out of here to get a few month's worth of sleep. Happy coding, everyone!

References

1 Sempé, Luis R. "Sky Domes." October 2001.
http://www.spheregames.com/files/SkyDomesPDF.zip.

2 Laeuchli, Jesse. "Programming Fractals." *Game Programming Gems 2*. Hingham, Massachusetts: Charles River Media, 2001. 239–246.

APPENDIX

WHAT'S ON THE CD

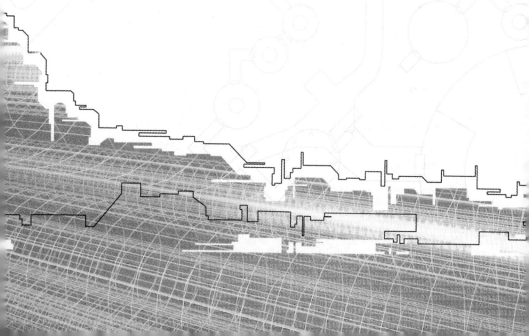

This book's accompanying CD-ROM contains lots of cool stuff that I encourage you to take a look at. I spent a few days compiling a series of demos and algorithm whitepapers to put on this CD, so make sure you look at everything.

The GUI

The CD-ROM's Graphical User Interface (GUI) is HTML based. It allows you to access the CD's various items and features quickly and easily. Most popular Web browsers can view this GUI, but your best bet is to view it with Netscape 4.0 (or later) or Internet Explorer 4.0 (or later). It's a pretty neat GUI if I do say so myself, so check it out and enjoy the pure GUI goodness that it presents.

System Requirements

The demos that accompany this CD are what I'm focusing my system requirements on, so keep that in mind. These demos aren't anything that an old Pentium 1 75MHz can run, but they don't require a state-of-the-art computer, either. Here are the minimum requirements that the demos on this book require:

- **CPU.** A 450MHz processor is required.
- **RAM.** A minimum of 64MB of RAM is required, but 128MB of RAM is recommended.
- **Graphics card.** A video card with at least 16MB of RAM is needed to run these demos. I would strongly recommend a 32MB Geforce 2 (or equivalent) or greater, however.
- **CD-ROM, DVD-ROM, CD-R, CD-RW, or DVD-RW drive.** Any one of these is needed. (How else do you expect to get the CD into the computer?)
- **Hard drive.** To copy everything from the CD to your hard drive would require a minimum of about 125MB of free space, but this really isn't needed. For users who just want to copy the algorithm whitepapers and the book's demo/code files, about 50MB of free space is needed, plus more for any of the accompanying demos that you would like to install.

Installation

I figured I'd put this section before the nitty-gritty details of the CD are presented. That way, you can just skip over them if you feel inclined to do so and simply check out the CD immediately. Installation of this CD is quite easy. If you have Windows 95 or later and you have the CD autorun feature enabled, the CD's menu should pop up right in front of your face, and you can get started exploring the CD! If the menu does not pop up, then you'll need to bring it up manually. To do this, go to My Computer and double-click (or single-click, depending on your computer's settings) on the CD's icon. If that still doesn't work, you need to get yourself to the CD's directory and double-click (or single-click) the start_here.htm file.

You should be able to navigate your way around the menu from this point on. If you experience any other problems with the CD, feel free to e-mail me at trent@codershq.com.

The Structure

The CD contains three main folders from which you can access the main components of the CD. These folders are as follows:

- **Algorithm Whitepapers.** These are where you can find the official documentation behind the three main terrain algorithms presented in this book. There is also a tutorial on texture generation and an in-depth analysis of the original ROAM algorithm.
- **Code.** This is where you can find the demos and code from the chapters in this book. All of the demos include a pre-built EXE, all the necessary files, and a Microsoft Visual C++ 6.0 workspace so that you can quickly load the demo into VC++ and compile it.
- **Demos.** This directory contains five demos. Two of these demos show off a terrain implementation of some kind (a voxel engine and a chunked LOD engine). There are also three demos that show how a terrain engine can be used in a game. One of these games is the impressive *TreadMarks*. In addition, you'll find a demo of Paint Shop Pro 7, in case you don't have a Paint program on your computer that is capable of reading TGA and RAW files. Do yourself a favor and check out these demos!

Index

GAME DEVELOPMENT.
IT'S SERIOUS BUSINESS.

"Game programming is without a doubt the most intellectually challenging field of Computer Science in the world. However, we would be fooling ourselves if we said that we are 'serious' people! Writing (and reading) a game programming book should be an exciting adventure for both the author and the reader."

—André LaMothe,
Series Editor

Gamedev.net

The most comprehensive game development resource

- The latest news in game development
- The most active forums and chatrooms anywhere, with insights and tips from experienced game developers
- Links to thousands of additional game development resources
- Thorough book and product reviews
- Over 1000 game development articles!
- Game design
- Graphics
- DirectX
- OpenGL
- AI
- Art
- Music
- Physics
- Source Code
- Sound
- Assembly
- And More!

 Gamedev.net

TAKE YOUR
GAME TO THE
XTREME!

Xtreme Games LLC was founded to help small game developers around the world create and publish their games on the commercial market. Xtreme Games helps younger developers break into the field of game programming by insulating them from complex legal and business issues. Xtreme Games has hundreds of developers around the world. If you're interested in becoming one of them, then visit us at **www.xgames3d.com.**

www.xgames3d.com

License Agreement/Notice of Limited Warranty

By opening the sealed disc container in this book, you agree to the following terms and conditions. If, upon reading the following license agreement and notice of limited warranty, you cannot agree to the terms and conditions set forth, return the unused book with unopened disc to the place where you purchased it for a refund.

License:
The enclosed software is copyrighted by the copyright holder(s) indicated on the software disc. You are licensed to copy the software onto a single computer for use by a single user and to a backup disc. You may not reproduce, make copies, or distribute copies or rent or lease the software in whole or in part, except with written permission of the copyright holder(s). You may transfer the enclosed disc only together with this license, and only if you destroy all other copies of the software and the transferee agrees to the terms of the license. You may not decompile, reverse assemble, or reverse engineer the software.

Notice of Limited Warranty:
The enclosed disc is warranted by Premier Press, Inc. to be free of physical defects in materials and workmanship for a period of sixty (60) days from end user's purchase of the book/disc combination. During the sixty-day term of the limited warranty, Premier Press will provide a replacement disc upon the return of a defective disc.

Limited Liability:
THE SOLE REMEDY FOR BREACH OF THIS LIMITED WARRANTY SHALL CONSIST ENTIRELY OF REPLACEMENT OF THE DEFECTIVE DISC. IN NO EVENT SHALL PREMIER PRESS OR THE AUTHORS BE LIABLE FOR ANY OTHER DAMAGES, INCLUDING LOSS OR CORRUPTION OF DATA, CHANGES IN THE FUNCTIONAL CHARACTERISTICS OF THE HARDWARE OR OPERATING SYSTEM, DELETERIOUS INTERACTION WITH OTHER SOFTWARE, OR ANY OTHER SPECIAL, INCIDENTAL, OR CONSEQUENTIAL DAMAGES THAT MAY ARISE, EVEN IF PREMIER AND/OR THE AUTHORS HAVE PREVIOUSLY BEEN NOTIFIED THAT THE POSSIBILITY OF SUCH DAMAGES EXISTS.

Disclaimer of Warranties:
PREMIER AND THE AUTHORS SPECIFICALLY DISCLAIM ANY AND ALL OTHER WARRANTIES, EITHER EXPRESS OR IMPLIED, INCLUDING WARRANTIES OF MERCHANTABILITY, SUITABILITY TO A PARTICULAR TASK OR PURPOSE, OR FREEDOM FROM ERRORS. SOME STATES DO NOT ALLOW FOR EXCLUSION OF IMPLIED WARRANTIES OR LIMITATION OF INCIDENTAL OR CONSEQUEN-TIAL DAMAGES, SO THESE LIMITATIONS MIGHT NOT APPLY TO YOU.

Other:
This Agreement is governed by the laws of the State of Indiana without regard to choice of law principles. The United Convention of Contracts for the International Sale of Goods is specifically disclaimed. This Agreement constitutes the entire agreement between you and Premier Press regarding use of the software.